STATUS OF WOMEN IN INDEPENDENT INDIA

Status of Women in Independent India

By

Sharat Dwivedi

2008

CYBER TECH PUBLICATIONS
4264/3, Ansari Road, Daryaganj, New Delhi-110002 (India)
Ph.: 011-23244078. Fax: 011-23280028
E-Mail: cyberpublicationsdelhi@yahoo.com

STATUS OF WOMEN IN INDEPENDENT INDIA

Sharat Dwivedi

First Edition 2008

Published by :

G.S. Rawat for **Cyber Tech Publications**
4264/3, Ansari Road, Daryaganj, New Delhi-110002 (India)
Ph.: 011-23244078. Fax: 011-23280028
E-Mail: cyberpublicationsdelhi@yahoo.com

Printed at : **Amit Enterprises**, Maujpur, Delhi, (9810878184)

Preface

Gender discrimination has been a universal phenomenon in human history from time immemorial. On account of her biological constitution, social taboos and scriptural sanction, the social position of the woman has always been considered as inferior and subordinate to man in society. No doubt the reformers brought great relief to the sufferings of the Indian women, but the social transformation could not cross religious boundaries. However, with the dawn of modern age, old values have changed. With new awareness on account of education, economic development, social awareness, social organisations, industrialisation, urbanisation, disintegration of joint families, economic and technical developments, pressures of consumer society, more opportunities for work, development of means of communication and transportation and social mobility, a great change has occurred in the attitude towards women. Subsequently, the position of women has certainly been enhanced.

Women have now certainly got a status in society. Although women have joined almost every profession in our country and most of them are doing excellent work. But everything does not stop there. She has to fight hard to retain her position and make people realise the worth of her skills. Economic independence is essential for the personality development of woman and for providing economic support to her family. It gives her confidence, liberty, identity, security, a status and a feeling of sharing the economic needs of the household. Much work is needed on the social front for the harmonious development of the position of women in our society.

Social evils like girl abuse, women abuse, dowry deaths, sati, gender discrimination etc are painful realities of our society. We have to deal with these problems seriously and sincerely. The dominant nature of the male in our society is one of the major factors to be sublimated to the spirit of equality. Girls should not be considered an unwanted burden, liability and problem. They need equal attention and loving treatment for the mental and physical development of their personality. Women should have more facilities for education, applied sciences, professional courses and training and more career prospects and avenues of employment.

We need more opportunities for the development of women entrepreneurship in the socio-economic, industrial and commercial spheres so that women can play a definite role in the economic development of the country and contribute significantly in the task of nation building. Although she has to awaken to her potentialities, she still needs more awareness and alertness about her rights and duties. She has definitely a serious role to play in the 21st century.

Present book deals with all the issues about the women and their role and status in the independent India.

—Author

Contents

1

INTRODUCTION

The status of women in India has been subject to great many changes over the past few millennia. From a largely unknown status in ancient times through the low points of the medieval period, to the promotion of equal rights by many reformers, the history of women in India has been eventful.

WOMEN IN ANCIENT INDIA

It is said that women enjoyed equal status with men in all fields of life in ancient India. In the early Vedic period women were educated. We can see this in the works of Grammarians such as 'Patanjali' & 'Katyayana'. Women got married at a mature age and were also free to select their husbands. Scriptures such as Rig Veda and Upanishads mention many women sages and seers, notably Gargi and Maitreyi.

There are some kingdoms in ancient India, which had customs such as 'nagarvadhu' i.e. the bride of the city. According to this custom women competed to win the prestigious title of 'nagarvadhu'. Amrapali is the most famous example of a 'nagarvadhu'. Women in fact had superior position than their male counterparts. It is truly in this period that women were really treated as Durga and Parvati.

There was a special thread ceremony in which girls were tied threads of honour based on merit. Later this ceremony was replaced by 'child-marriage'. Child-Marriage by this time was started on a large scale because of many holy books. Girls were married when they were infants.

They were send to their husbands house when they attained puberty. Girls were not permitted to gain education. Although many Jain institutions admitted girls but it was of no use as only few number of girls attended these institutes.

WOMEN IN MEDIEVAL INDIA

The condition of Women in society was deteriorated more during the medieval period. At this point of time child-marriage, sati, female infanticide was practiced largely. The Muslim seclusion in India introduced the 'purdah' system by and large on Muslim women. These women were also forced to practice 'zenana'.

The Rajput women of Rajasthan who are known to place a high premium on honour practiced 'jauhar'. Jauhar refers to the practice of the voluntary immolation of all the wives and daughters of defeated warriors, in order to avoid capture and consequent molestation by the enemy. Polygamy i.e. husband marrying more than once was practised by most Hindu Kshatriyas. At the same time many women excelled in arts, literature, music. Women were also rulers in the medival period. Some of the great women rulers were Razia Sultan, the only women monarch to rule the throne of Delhi.

The Gond queen Durgavati ruled for fifteen long years, before she lost the battle to mughal emperor Akbar's general Asaf Ali. Chand Bibi also fought the mughals in 1590's. Nur Jehan the only mughal women ruler is still today considered the most effective ruler.

Inspite of all these successful women the condition of a poor Indian women was the same. At this time, girls were married at an early age say 5-6 years. Sati was also practised where women were forced to jump in the burning funeral of their dead husband.

Purdah was practised among muslim women i.e. to cover their heads fully with a 'veil'. Devdasi was prevalent in south India where girls were married to deity or trees. This practise had destoyed the lives of many girls as they were physically molested and sexually exploited by many pundits.

WOMEN IN MODERN INDIA

Modern India wittnessed improvements in the Status of Women There were many women reformers who worked for the betterment and upliftment of their other female counterparts.The begum of Bhopal discarded the purdah and fought in the revolt of 1857.

Many reformers like Ishwarchandra Vidyasagar, Jyotiba Phule with his wife Savitribai Phule undertook various measures to eradicate social stigmas from the society. Sir Sayyed Ahmad Khan established the Aligarh Muslim University for the spread of education among the Muslims. He also abolished the purdah system among muslim women. Many Acts were passed for the upliftment of women among those Widow Remarraige Act of 1856 was important.

In the modern times, Indian women were given liberties and rights such as freedom of expression and equality, as well as right to get education. But still today, we are fighting for crisis such as dowry, female infanticide, sex selective abortions, health, domestic violence, etc. Women today are educated but illiterate in terms of knowing their rights properly.Another harmful practise is the Dowry system where gift of money or valuables given by the bride's family to the groom's at the time of their marriage. This is the new harrasment in the name of wedding gift. Women are killed if they bring less dowry after marriage. The term Bride Burning is criticized within India itself.

India has a low sex ratio, the chief reason being that many child die before reaching adulthood.They are aboted in the womb itself as many people do not want a girl child because they cannot pay dowry.

This is a vicious circle which is linked to one another.It is somewhere a criticism that highest female ratio lies in Kerala and Tribal societies in India knowing the fact that tribal communities have far lower levels of income, literacy and health facilities.Female infanticide (killing of girl infants) is still prevalent in some rural areas. Dowry has been one of the main reasons for female infanticides in India.

The level of Domestic violence is also high in India.Husbands beat their wifes in a drunken state to get rid of their frustration. Domestic violence is also prevalent because of 'dowry'. Trafficking is also a big reason for female abuse. Trafficking means girls are sold to big people for satisfying their sexual needs or kidnapped to make them prostitutes. In many rural families, girls and women face nutritional discrimination within the family, and are anaemic and malnourished.

The maternal mortality in India is the second highest in the world. Only a few percentage of births in the country are supervised by doctors. Most women deliver with the help of traditional nurses in the village who often lack the skills and resources to save the mother's life if it is in danger. Women suffer many health problems because of abuse and other mal-nourishments. The average Indian woman has little control over her own fertility and reproductive health. So women today in short are suffering from various other problems but still thanks to the reformer's like Jyotiba Phule, Dayanand Saraswati, Swami Vivekanand that they still can live to an extent on their own & fight for their Rights

CHRONIC HUNGER AND WOMEN IN INDIA

Introductory Quotes

You can tell the condition of a nation by looking at the status of its women. — *Jawaharlal Nehru*

However much a mother may love her children, it is all but impossible for her to provide high-quality child care if she herself is poor and oppressed, illiterate and uninformed, anaemic and unhealthy, has five or six other children, lives in a slum or shanty, has neither clean water nor safe sanitation, and if she is without the necessary support either from health services, or from her society, or from the father of her childen.
— *Vulimiri Ramalingaswami, "The Asian Enigma"*

The women who participate in and lead ecology movements in countries like India are not speaking merely as victims. Their voices are the voices of liberation

and transformation... The women's and ecology movements are therefore one, and are primarily counter-trends to a patriarchal maldevelopment.

— Vandana Shiva

Amartya Sen-The Unheeded Conscience: We will lionise him, but will we ever listen to what he's saying?

Sen points out that when he took up issues of women's welfare, he was accused in India of voicing "foreign concerns." "I was told Indian women don't think like that about equality. But I would like to argue that if they don't think like that they should be given a real opportunity to think like that."

— Parmita Shastri, Outlook India, 1998

The persistence of hunger and abject poverty in India and other parts of the world is due in large measure to the subjugation, marginalization and disempowerment of women. Women suffer from hunger and poverty in greater numbers and to a great degree then men. At the same time, it is women who bear the primary responsibility for actions needed to end hunger: education, nutrition, health and family income.

Looking through the lens of hunger and poverty, there are seven major areas of discrimination against women in India:

- *Malnutrition*: India has exceptionally high rates of child malnutrition, because tradition in India requires that women eat last and least throughout their lives, even when pregnant and lactating. Malnourished women give birth to malnourished children, perpetuating the cycle.
- *Poor Health*: Females receive less health care than males. Many women die in childbirth of easily prevented complications. Working conditions and environmental pollution further impairs women's health.
- *Lack of education*: Families are far less likely to educate girls than boys, and far more likely to pull them out of school, either to help out at home or from fear of violence.
- *Overwork*: Women work longer hours and their work is more arduous than men's, yet their work is unrecognized.

Men report that "women, like children, eat and do nothing." Technological progress in agriculture has had a negative impact on women.

- *Unskilled*: In women's primary employment sector-agriculture-extension services overlook women.
- *Mistreatment*: In recent years, there has been an alarming rise in atrocities against women in India, in terms of rapes, assaults and dowry-related murders. Fear of violence suppresses the aspirations of all women. Female infanticide and sex-selective abortions are additional forms of violence that reflect the devaluing of females in Indian society.
- *Powerlessness*: While women are guaranteed equality under the constitution, legal protection has little effect in the face of prevailing patriarchal traditions. Women lack power to decide who they will marry, and are often married off as children. Legal loopholes are used to deny women inheritance rights.

India has a long history of activism for women's welfare and rights, which has increasingly focused on women's economic rights. A range of government programs have been launched to increase economic opportunity for women, although there appear to be no existing programs to address the cultural and traditional discrimination against women that leads to her abject conditions.

THE INEXTRICABLE LINK

The greatest tragedy facing humanity today is the persistence of chronic hunger-an intolerable phenomenon that takes the lives of 24,000 of us every day. For fully one-fifth of humanity, life is a daily struggle to survive in conditions of relentless poverty. Day after day, the lives of one billion individuals are cut short or terribly diminished by chronic, persistent hunger. Day after day, one billion people are denied the opportunities they need to lead healthy and productive lives.

People living with chronic hunger exist in conditions of severe poverty. What they lack is the chance to change their situation, to develop their own self-sufficiency. The most potent confirmation of this fact can be seen in the lives of women. They, along with their children, are the main victims of hunger, and they are also most lacking in opportunities to end their own and their families' hunger.

The Hunger Project has come to the recognition that the persistence of hunger in India-and elsewhere in the world where hunger is still an overriding social issue-is, to a large degree, due to the subjugation, marginalization and disempowerment of women. Furthermore, women's suppression is rooted in the very fabric of Indian society-in traditions, in religious doctrine and practices, within the educational and legal systems, and within families.

Ironically, much of the essential work of ending hunger rests in women's hands.

Traditionally, women bear primary responsibility for the well-being of their families. Yet they are systematically denied access to the resources they need to fulfill their responsibility, which includes education, health care services, job training, and access and freedom to use family planning services.

In order to gain a shared understanding of the condition of the status of women in India and its impact on the persistence of hunger, this document surveys papers done by leading scholars in Indian development issues.

It is organized in a framework of seven issues that characterize the plight of resource-poor women, with a focus on rural women, in India: malnutrition, poor health, lack of education, overwork, lack of skills, mistreatment and powerlessness.

The link between these issues and the persistence of hunger in India was underscored in a 1996 study: The Asian Enigma, by Vulimiri Ramalingaswami:

> *In short, the poor care that is afforded to girls and women by their husbands and by elders is the first major reason for levels of child malnutrition that are markedly higher in South Asia than anywhere else in the world.*

INDIA: AN OVERVIEW

India, with a population of 989 million, is the world's second most populous country. Of that number, 120 million are women who live in poverty.

India has 16 percent of the world's population, but only 2.4 percent of its land, resulting in great pressures on its natural resources.

Over 70 percent of India's population currently derive their livelihood from land resources, which includes 84 percent of the economically-active women.

India is one of the few countries where males significantly outnumber females, and this imbalance has increased over time. India's maternal mortality rates in rural areas are among the world's highest. From a global perspective, Indian accounts for 19 percent of all lives births and 27 percent of all maternal deaths.

"There seems to be a consensus that higher female mortality between ages one and five and high maternal mortality rates result in a deficit of females in the population. Chatterjee (1990) estimates that deaths of young girls in India exceed those of young boys by over 300,000 each year, and every sixth infant death is specifically due to gender discrimination." Of the 15 million baby girls born in India each year, nearly 25 percent will not live to see their 15th birthday.

> *"Although India was the first country to announce an official family planning program in 1952, its population grew from 361 million in 1951 to 844 million in 1991. India's total fertility rate of 3.8 births per woman can be considered moderate by world standards, but the sheer magnitude of population increase has resulted in such a feeling of urgency that containment of population growth is listed as one of the six most important objectives in the Eighth Five-Year Plan."*

Since 1970, the use of modern contraceptive methods has risen from 10 percent to 40 percent, with great variance between northern and southern India. The most striking aspect of contraceptive use in India is the predominance of sterilization, which accounts for more than 85 percent of total modern contraception use, with female sterilization accounting for 90 percent of all sterilizations.

The Indian constitution grants women equal rights with men, but strong patriarchal traditions persist, with women's lives shaped by customs that are centuries old. In most Indian families, a daughter is viewed as a liability, and she is conditioned to believe that she is inferior and subordinate to men. Sons are idolized and celebrated. May you be the mother of a hundred sons is a common Hindu wedding blessing.

The origin of the Indian idea of appropriate female behavior can be traced to the rules laid down by Manu in 200 B.C.: "by a young girl, by a young woman, or even by an aged one, nothing must be done independently, even in her own house". "In childhood a female must be subject to her father, in youth to her husband, when her lord is dead to her sons; a woman must never be independent."

A study of women in the Swayam Shikshan Prayog (SSP), based in 20 villages in four districts in Maharashtra state was introduced in this way:

The primary issue all women in the SSP were struggling with was that of everyday survival. Insufficient incomes and the lack of employment were reported to be their most pressing concerns. Survival is a constant preoccupation and at its most basic, survival means food (Chambers 1983). The most common problems were the lack of basic amenities such as food, water, fuel, fodder and health facilities.

In addition, the deterioration of the natural environment and the fact that many of their traditional occupations were no longer viable were conditions that were making it increasingly hard for women to continue sustaining their families, as they had done in the past.

SSP is a loose, informal network of women's collectives, voluntary organizations, action groups and unions.

Women are Malnourished

The exceptionally high rates of malnutrition in South Asia are rooted deeply in the soil of inequality between men and women.

> *"...the poor care that is afforded to girls and women by their husbands and by elders is the first major reason for levels of child malnutrition that are markedly higher in South Asia than anywhere else in the world."*

This point is made in the article, The Asian Enigma, published by UNICEF in the 1996 Progress of Nations, in which the rates of childhood malnutrition in South Asia are compared with those in Africa. We learn that malnutrition is far worse in South Asia, directly due to the fact that women in South Asia have less voice and freedom of movement than in Africa. "Judgement and self-expression and independence largely denied, millions of women in South Asia have neither the knowledge nor the means nor the freedom to act in their own and their children's best interests."

> *"Gender disparities in nutrition are evident from infancy to adulthood. In fact, gender has been the most statistically significant determinant of malnutrition among young children and malnutrition is a frequent direct or underlying cause of death among girls below age 5. Girls are breast-fed less frequently and for shorter durations in infancy; in childhood and adulthood, males are fed first and better. Adult women consume approximately 1,000 fewer calories per day than men according to one estimate from Punjab. Comparison of household dietary intake studies in different parts of the country shows that nutritional equity between males and females is lower in northern than in southern states."*

Nutritional deprivation has two major consequences for women: they never reach their full growth potential and anaemia. Both are risk factors in pregnancy, with anaemia ranging from 40-50 percent in urban areas to 50-70 percent in rural areas. This condition complicates childbearing and result in maternal and infant deaths, and low birth weight infants.

One study found anaemia in over 95 percent of girls ages 6-14 in Calcutta, around 67 percent in the Hyderabad area, 73 percent in the New Delhi area, and about 18 percent in the Madras area. This study states, "The prevalence of anaemia among women ages 15-24 and 25-44 years follows similar patterns and levels. Besides posing risks during pregnancy, anaemia increases women's susceptibility to diseases such as tuberculosis and reduces the energy women have available for daily activities such as household chores, child care, and agricultural labor. Any severely anaemic individual is taxed by most physical activities, including walking at an ordinary pace.

Women are in Poor Health

Surviving through a normal life cycle is a resource-poor woman's greatest challenge.

> *"The practice of breast-feeding female children for shorter periods of time reflects the strong desire for sons. If women are particularly anxious to have a male child, they may deliberately try to become pregnant again as soon as possible after a female is born. Conversely, women may consciously seek to avoid another pregnancy after the birth of a male child in order to give maximum attention to the new son."*

A primary way that parents discriminate against their girl children is through neglect during illness. When sick, little girls are not taken to the doctor as frequently as are their brothers. A study in Punjab shows that medical expenditures for boys are 2.3 times higher than for girls.

As adults, women get less health care than men. They tend to be less likely to admit that they are sick and they'll wait until their sickness has progressed before they seek help or help is sought for them. Studies on attendance at rural primary health centers reveal that more males than females are treated in almost all parts of the country, with differences greater in northern hospitals than southern ones, pointing to regional differences in the value placed on women. Women's socialization to tolerate suffering and their reluctance to be examined by male personnel are additional constraints in their getting adequate health care.

MATERNAL MORTALITY

India's maternal mortality rates in rural areas are among the highest in the world.

A factor that contributes to India's high maternal mortality rate is the reluctance to seek medical care for pregnancy-it is viewed as a temporary condition that will disappear. The estimates nationwide are that only 40-50 percent of women receive any antenatal care. Evidence from the states of Bihar, Rajasthan, Orissa, Uttar Pradesh, Maharashtra and Gujarat find registration for maternal and child health services to be as low as 5-22 percent in rural areas and 21-51 percent in urban areas.

Even a woman who has had difficulties with previous pregnancies is usually treated with home remedies only for three reasons: the decision that a pregnant woman seek help rests with the mother-in-law and husband; financial considerations; and fear that the treatment may be more harmful than the malady.

It is estimated that pregnancy-related deaths account for one-quarter of all fatalities among women aged 15 to 29, with well over two-thirds of them considered preventable. For every maternal death in India, an estimated 20 more women suffer from impaired health. One village-level study of rural women in Maharashtra determined on the basis of physical examinations that some 92 percent suffered from one or more gynecological disorder.

CONTRACEPTION USE

Women's health is harmed by lack of access to and the poor quality of reproductive services.

> *"About 24.6 million couples, representing roughly 18 percent of all married women, want no more children but are not using contraception. (Operations Research Group, 1990). The causes of this unmet need remain*

> *poorly understood, but a qualitative study in Tamil Nadu suggests that women's lack of decision-making power in the family, opportunity costs involved in seeking contraception, fear of child death, and poor quality of contraceptive service all play an important role." (Ravindran 1993).*

Some estimates suggest that some 5 million abortions are performed annually in India, with the large majority being illegal. As a result, abortion-related mortality is high. Although abortion has been legal since 1972 in India, "studies suggest that although official policy seeks to make pregnancy-termination services widely available, in practice guidelines on abortion limit access to services, particularly in rural areas. In 1981, of the 6,200 physicians trained to perform abortions, only 1,600 were working in rural areas."

JOB IMPACT ON MATERNAL HEALTH

Working conditions result in premature and stillbirths.

The tasks performed by women are usually those that require them to be in one position for long periods of time, which can adversely affect their reproductive health. A study in a rice-growing belt of coastal Maharashtra found that 40 percent of all infant deaths occurred in the months of July to October. The study also found that a majority of births were either premature or stillbirths. The study attributed this to the squatting position that had to be assumed during July and August, the rice transplanting months.

IMPACT OF POLLUTION ON WOMEN

Women's health is further harmed by air and water pollution and lack of sanitation.

The impact of pollution and industrial wastes on health is considerable. In Environment, Development and the Gender Gap, Sandhya Venkateswaran asserts that "the high incidence of malnutrition present amongst women and their low metabolism and other health problems affect their capacity to deal with chemical stress. The smoke from household biomass (made up of wood, dung and crop residues) stoves within a three-hour period is equivalent to smoking 20 packs of cigarettes. For women who spend at least three hours per day cooking, often in a poorly ventilated area, the impact includes eye problems, respiratory problems, chronic bronchitis and lung cancer. One study quoted by WHO in 1991 found that pregnant women cooking over open biomass stoves had almost a 50 percent higher chance of stillbirth.

Anaemia makes a person more susceptible to carbon monoxide toxicity, which is one of the main pollutants in the biomass smoke. Given the number of Indian women who are anaemic-25 to 30 percent in the reproductive age group and almost 50 percent in the third trimester-this adds to their vulnerability to carbon monoxide toxicity.

Additionally, with an increasing population, diseases caused by waste disposal, such as hookworm, are rampant. People who work barefooted are particularly susceptible, and it has been found that hookworm is directly responsible for the high percentage of anaemia among rural women.

Women are Uneducated

Women and girls receive far less education than men, due both to social norms and fears of violence. India has the largest population of non-school-going working girls.

India's constitution guarantees free primary school education for both boys and girls up to age 14. This goal has been repeatedly reconfirmed, but primary education in India is not universal. Overall, the literacy rate for women is 39 percent versus 64 percent for men. The rate for women in the four large northern states-Bihar, Uttar Pradesh, Rajasthan and Madhya Pradesh-is lower than the national average: it was 25 percent in 1991. Attendance rates from the 1981 census suggest that no more than 1/3 of all girls (and a lower proportion of rural girls) aged 5-14 are attending school.

Although substantial progress has been achieved since India won its independence in 1947, when less than 8 percent of females were literate, the gains have not been rapid enough to keep pace with population growth: there were 16 million more illiterate females in 1991 than in 1981.

Sonalde Desai in Gender Inequalities and Demographic Behavior asserts that "parents' reluctance to educate daughters has its roots in the situation of women. Parents have several incentives for not educating their daughters. Foremost is the view that education of girls brings no returns to parents and that their future roles, being mainly reproductive and perhaps including agricultural labor, require no formal education. As more and more boys are engaged in education, there is a growing reliance on the labor of girls. Girls are increasingly replacing their brothers on the farm while carrying on their usual responsibilities in housework. A large proportion of the roughly 40 million "nonworking" girls who are not in school are kept at home because of responsibilities in housework."

The role of parents is to deliver a chaste daughter to her husband's family. Sonalde Desai goes on to point out that "another disincentive for sending daughters to school is a concern for the protection of their virginity. When schools are located at a distance, when teachers are male, and when girls are expected to study along with boys, parents are often unwilling to expose their daughters to the potential assault on their virginity."

There is little response to counter these obstacles: school hours remain inflexible to the labor demands of girls; many villages do not have a school; and fewer than 1/3 of India's primary and middle-school teachers are women.

According to Mapping Progress, "educational funds were cut by 801.3 million rupees in the 1991-92 budget. Funds for the mass literacy movement, in which women participate enthusiastically, have been reduced by 5 percent from the previous year. Budgetary provisions for non-formal education have been cut by 17 percent, leading to closure of many night schools and adult education programs in which working-class women participate. Reduction in government expenditures on higher education and encouragement to private colleges will reduce women's opportunities for higher education since privatization in education promotes only male-dominated professional and technical courses, as they are lucrative."

Women are Overworked

Women work longer hours and their work is more arduous than men's. Still, men report that "women, like children, eat and do nothing."

Hours Worked

Women work roughly twice as many as many hours as men. Women's contribution to agriculture-whether it be subsistence farming or commercial agriculture-when measured in terms of the number of tasks performed and time spent, is greater than men. "The extent of women's contribution is aptly highlighted by a micro study conducted in the Indian Himalayas which found that on a one-hectare farm, a pair of bullocks works 1,064 hours, a man 1,212 hours and a woman 3,485 hours in a year."

In Andhra Pradesh, (Mies 1986) found that the work day of an woman agricultural labourer during the agricultural season lasts for 15 hours, from 4 am to 8 pm, with an hour's rest in between. Her male counterpart works for seven to eight hours, from 5 am to 10 am or 11 am and from 3 pm to 5 pm.

Another study on time and energy spent by men and women on agricultural work (Batliwala 1982) found that 53 percent of the total human hours per household are contributed by women as compared to 31 percent by men. The remaining contribution comes from children.

The linking of agricultural activities to male dominance is described by Roy Burman (in Menon 1991):

> *The anxiety of man to monopolize his skill in plough culture is reflected in the taboo that is observed almost all over India, against the women's handling the plough. In many societies, she is not even allowed to touch it.*

Mies further observed that "whereas operations performed by men were those that entailed the use of machinery and draught animals, thereby using animal, hydraulic, mechanical or electrical energy, women almost always relied on manual labour, using only their own energy." Rice transplantations, the most arduous and labour intensive task in rice cultivation, is carried out entirely by women without the help of any tools.

> *"Girls learn to assist their mothers in almost all tasks, and from the age of 10 years participate fully in the agricultural work done by women. Mies cites the case of Laxmi, a three-year-old infant who, along with her mother, pulled seedlings for transplanting. Boys on the other hand were seldom seen transplanting or weeding though they did help out in ploughing or watering the fields."*

"Not only do women perform more tasks, their work is also more arduous than that undertaken by men. Both transplantation and weeding require women to spend the whole day and work in muddy soil with their hands. Moreover, they work the entire day under the intensely hot sun while men's work, such as ploughing and watering the fields, is invariably carried out early in the morning before the sun gets too hot. Mies argues that because women's work, unlike men's, does not involve implements and is based largely on human energy, it is considered unskilled and hence less productive. On this basis, women are invariably paid lower wages, despite the fact that they work harder and for longer hours than do men."

In contrast, a study in Uttar Pradesh reports that men "only reluctantly conceded that their womenfolk really work. The researchers in this area were repeatedly told that women, like children, simply eat food and do nothing."

THE INVISIBILITY OF WOMEN'S WORK

Women's work is rarely recognized.

Many maintain that women's economic dependence on men impacts their power within the family. With increased participation in income-earning activities, not only will there be more income for the family, but gender inequality should be reduced. This issue is particularly salient in India because studies show a very low level of female participation in the labor force. This under-reporting is attributed to the frequently held view that women's work is not economically productive.

In a report of the National Commission on Self-Employed Women and Women in the Informal Sector, the director of social welfare in one state said, "There are no women in any unorganized sector in our state." When the Commission probed and asked, "Are there any women who go to the forest to collect firewood? Do any of the women in rural areas have cattle?" the director responded with, "Of course, there are many women doing that type of work." Working women are invisible to most of the population.

If all activities-including maintenance of kitchen gardens and poultry, grinding food grains, collecting water and firewood, etc.-are taken into account, then 88 percent of rural housewives and 66 percent of urban housewives can be considered as economically productive.

Women's employment in family farms or businesses is rarely recognized as economically productive, either by men or women. And, any income generated from this work is generally controlled by the men. Such work is unlikely to increase women's participation in allocating family finances. In a 1992 study of family-based texile workers, male children who helped in a home-based handloom mill were given pocket money, but the adult women and girls were not.

THE IMPACT OF TECHNOLOGY ON WOMEN

The shift from subsistence to a market economy has a dramatic negative impact on women.

According to Sandhya Venkateswaran, citing Shiva, the Green Revolution, which focused on increasing yields of rice and wheat, entailed a shift in inputs from human to technical. Women's participation, knowledge and inputs were marginalized, and their role shift from being "primary producers to subsidiary workers."

Where technology has been introduced in areas where women worked, women labourers have often been displaced by men. Threshing of grain was almost exclusively a female task, and with the introduction of automatic grain threshers-which are only operated by men-women have lost an important source of income.

Combine harvesters leave virtually no residue. This means that this source of fodder is no longer available to women, which has a dramatic impact on women's workload. So too, as cattle dung is being used as fertilizer, there is less available for fuel for cooking.

> *"Commercialization and the consequent focus on cash crops has led to a situation where food is lifted straight from the farm to the market. The income accrued is controlled by men. Earlier, most of the produce was brought home and stored, and the women exchanged it for other commodities. Such a system vested more control with the women."*

Women are Unskilled

Women have unequal access to resources. Extension services tend to reach only men, which perpetuates the existing division of labour in the agricultural sector, with women continuing to perform unskilled tasks. A World Bank study in 1991 reveals that the assumption made by extension workers is that information within a family will be transmitted to the women by the men, which in actual practice seldom happens. "The male dominated extension system tends to overlook women's role in agriculture and proves ineffective in providing technical information to women farmers."

Mapping Progress, states, "in the farm sector, the process of mechanization of agricultural activities has brought in tendencies for gender discrimination by replacing men for a number of activities performed by women and also by displacing the labor of women from subsistence and marginal households. Women are employed only when there is absolute shortage of labor and for specific operations like cotton-picking.

> *"To supply food-processing industries being set up with foreign collaboration, there has already been a major*

shift from subsistence farming method of rice, millet, corn and wheat to cash-crop production of fruit, mushrooms, flowers and vegetables. This shift has led to women being the first to lose jobs."

A number of factors perpetuate women's limited job skills: if training women for economic activities requires them to leave their village, this is usually a problem for them. Unequal access to education restricts women's abilities to learn skills that require even functional levels of literacy. In terms of skill development, women are impeded by their lack of mobility, low literacy levels and prejudiced attitudes toward women. When women negotiate with banks and government officials, they are often ostracized by other men and women in their community for being 'too forward.' Government and bank officials have preconceived ideas of what women are capable of, and stereotypes of what is considered women's work.

Women are Mistreated

Violence against women and girls is the most pervasive human rights violation in the world today.

Opening the door on the subject of violence against the world's females is like standing at the threshold of an immense dark chamber vibrating with collective anguish, but with the sounds of protest throttled back to a murmur. Where there should be outrage aimed at an intolerable status quo there is instead denial, and the largely passive acceptance of 'the way things are.'

Male violence against women is a worldwide phenomenon. Although not every woman has experienced it, and many expect not to, fear of violence is an important factor in the lives of most women. It determines what they do, when they do it, where they do it, and with whom. Fear of violence is a cause of women's lack of participation in activities beyond the home, as well as inside it. Within the home, women and girls may be subjected to physical and sexual abuse as punishment or as culturally justified assaults. These acts shape their attitude to life, and their expectations of themselves.

The insecurity outside the household is today the greatest obstacle in the path of women. Conscious that, compared to the atrocities outside the house, atrocities within the house are endurable, women not only continued to accept their inferiority in the house and society, but even called it sweet.

In recent years, there has been an alarming rise in atrocities against women in India. Every 26 minutes a woman is molested. Every 34 minutes a rape takes place. Every 42 minutes a sexual harassment incident occurs. Every 43 minutes a woman is kidnapped. And every 93 minutes a woman is burnt to death over dowry.

One-quarter of the reported rapes involve girls under the age of 16 but the vast majority are never reported. Although the penalty is severe, convictions are rare.

Selective Abortions

The most extreme expression of the preference for sons is female infanticide and sex-selective abortion.

A study of amniocentesis in a Bombay hospital found that 96 percent of female fetuses were aborted, compared with only a small percentage of male fetuses.

> *"Government officials event suspect that the disproportionate abortion of female fetuses may be a major underlying cause of the recent decline in the nation's sex ratio. In 1971 there were 930 females for every 1,000 males. A decade later this figure had increased to 934, but by 1991, instead of continuing to rise, the ratio dropped to 927, lower than the 1971 figure. This sex ratio is one of the lowest in the world."*

Sonalda Desai reports that there are posters in Bombay advertising sex-determination tests that read, "It is better to pay 500 Rs. now than 50,000 Rs. (in dowry) later."

Government has passed legislation to curb the misuse of amniocentesis for sex selection and abortion of female fetuses. Women activists have been critical of this act because of its provision that calls for punishing the women who seek the procedure. These women may be under pressure to bear a male child.

Women are Powerless

Legal protection of women's rights have little effect in the face of prevailing patriarchal traditions.

Marriage: Women are subordinate in most marriages.

Exposure to and interactions with the outside world are instrumental in determining the possibilities available to women in their daily lives. The situation of women is affected by the degree of their autonomy or capacity to make decisions both inside and outside their own household.

> *"The position of women in northern India is notably poor. Traditional Hindu society in northern rural areas is hierarchical and dominated by men, as evidenced by marriage customs. North Indian Hindus are expected to marry within prescribed boundaries: the bride and groom must not be related, they have no say in the matter, and the man must live outside the woman's natal village."*

"Wife givers" are socially and ritually inferior to "wife takers", thus necessitating the provision of a dowry. After marriage, the bride moves in with her husband's family. Such a bride is "a stranger in a strange place." They are controlled by the older females in the household, and their behavior reflects on the honor of their husbands. Because emotional ties between spouses are considered a potential threat to the solidarity of the patrilineal group, the northern system tends to segregate the sexes and limit communication between spouses-a circumstance that has direct consequences for family planning and similar "modern" behaviors that affect health. A young Indian bride is brought up to believe that her own wishes and interests are subordinate to those of her husband and his family. The primary duty of a newly married young woman, and virtually her only means of improving her position in the hierarchy of her husband's household, is to bear sons."

Sonalde Desai points out that the perception that sons are the major source of economic security in old age is so strong in the north that "many parents, while visiting their married daughters, do not accept food or other hospitality from them. However, given women's low independent incomes and lack of control over their earnings, few can provide economic support to their parents even if parents were willing to accept it."

In the south, in contrast, a daughter traditionally marries her mother's brother or her mother's brother's son (her first cousin). Such an arrangement has a dramatic impact on women. "In southern India, men are likely to marry women to whom they are related, so that the strict distinction found in the north between patrilineal and marital relatives is absent. Women are likely to be married into family households near their natal homes, and are more likely to retain close relationships with their natal kin."

"Over the past several decades, however, marriage patterns have changed markedly. Social, economic, and demographic developments have made marriages between close relatives less common, and the bride price has given way to a dowry system akin to that in the north. Nevertheless, as long as the underlying ethic of marriage in the south remains the reinforcement of existing kinship ties, the relatively favorable situation of southern Indian women is unlikely to be threatened."

CHILD MARRIAGES

Child marriages keep women subjugated.

A 1976 amendment to the Child Marriage Restraint Act raised the minimum legal age for marriage from 15 to 18 for young women and from 18 to 21 for young men. However, in many rural communities, illegal child marriages are still common. In some rural areas, nearly half the girls between 10 and 14 are married. Because there is pressure on women to prove their fertility by conceiving as soon as possible after marriage, adolescent marriage is synonymous with adolescent childbearing: roughly 10-15 percent of all births take place to women in their teens.

A May 1998 article in the New York Times states: Child marriages contribute to virtually every social malaise that keeps India behind in women's rights. The problems include soaring birth rates, grinding poverty and malnutrition, high illiteracy and infant mortality and low life expectancy, especially among rural women.

The article cites a 1993 survey of more than 5,000 women in Rajasthan, which showed that 56 percent of them had married before they were 15. Barely 18 percent of them were literate and only 3 percent used any form of birth control other than sterilization. Sixty-three percent of the children under age 4 of these women were severely undernourished.

> *"Each year, formal warnings are posted outside state government offices stating that child marriages are illegal, but they have little impact."*

One man interviewed for the article has seven daughters. He borrowed some 60,000 rupees to pay for the dowries for six of his daughters, ranging in age from 4-14. He reported that "the weddings mean that he can now look forward to growing old without being trapped in the penury by the need to support his daughters." (NYT)

Dowries: Women are kept subordinate, and are even murdered, by the practice of dowry.

In India, 6,000 dowry murders are committed each year. This reality exists even though the Dowry Prohibition Act has been in existence for 33 years, and there are virtually no arrests under the Act. Since those giving as well as those accepting dowry are punishable under the existing law, no one is willing to complain.

It is only after a "dowry death" that the complaints become public. It is estimated that the average dowry today is equivalent to five times the family's annual income and that the high cost of weddings and dowries is a major cause of indebtedness among India's poor.

A December 1997 article in India Today, entitled, Victims of Sudden Affluence states, "A woman on fire has made dowry deaths the most vicious of social crimes; it is an evil endemic to the subcontinent but despite every attempt at justice the numbers have continued to climb. With get-rich-quick becoming the new mantra, dowry became the perfect instrument for upward material mobility."

A study done by a policy think-tank, the Institute of Development and Communication, states, "the quantum of dowry exchange may still be greater among the upper classes, but 80 percent of dowry deaths and 80 percent of dowry harassment occurs in the middle and lower stratas."

The article goes on to state, "So complete is the discrimination among women that the gender bias is extended even toward the guilty. In a bizarre trend, the onus of murder is often put on the women to protect the men. Sometimes it is by consent. Often, old mothers-in-law embrace all the blame to bail out their sons and husbands."

Despite every stigma, dowry continues to be the signature of marriage. Says Rainuka Dagar, "It is taken as a normative custom and dowry harassment as a part of family life."

Divorce: Divorce is not a viable option.

Divorce is rare-it is a considered a shameful admission of a woman's failure as a wife and daughter-in-law. In 1990, divorced women made up a miniscule 0.08 percent of the total female population.

Maintenance rights of women in the case of divorce are weak. Although both Hindu and Muslim law recognize the rights of women and children to maintenance, in practice, maintenance is rarely set at a sufficient amount and is frequently violated.

Both Hindu and Muslim personal laws fail to recognize matrimonial property. Upon divorce, women have no rights to their home or to other property accumulated during marriage; in effect, their contributions to the maintenance of the family and accumulation of family assets go unrecognized and unrewarded.

RIGHT TO INHERITANCE

Women's rights to inheritance are limited and frequently violated.

In the mid-1950s the Hindu personal laws, which apply to all Hindus, Buddhists, Sikhs and Jains, were overhauled, banning polygamy and giving women rights to inheritance, adoption and divorce. The Muslim personal laws differ considerably from that of the Hindus, and permit polygamy. Despite various laws protecting women's rights, traditional patriarchal attitudes still prevail and are strengthened and perpetuated in the home.

Under Hindu law, sons have an independent share in the ancestral property. However, daughters' shares are based on the share received by their father. Hence, a father can effectively disinherit a daughter by renouncing his share of the ancestral property, but the son will continue to have a share in his own right. Additionally, married daughters, even those facing marital harassment, have no residential rights in the ancestral home.

Even the weak laws protecting women have not been adequately enforced. As a result, in practice, women continue to have little access to land and property, a major source of income and long-term economic security. Under the pretext of preventing fragmentation of agricultural holdings, several states have successfully excluded widows and daughters from inheriting agricultural land.

Women in Public Office (Revised May, 1999)

Panchayat Raj Institutions

The highest national priority must be the unleashing of woman power in governance. That is the single most important source of societal energy that we have kept corked for half a century.

— Mani Shankar Aiyar, journalist, India Today

Through the experience of the Indian Panchayat Raj Institutions (PRI) 1 million women have actively entered political life in India. The 73rd and 74th Constitutional Amendment Acts, which guarantee that all local elected bodies reserve one-third of their seats for women, have spearheaded an unprecedented social experiment which is playing itself out in more than 500,000 villages that are home to more than 600 million people.

Since the creation of the quota system, local women-the vast majority of them illiterate and poor-have come to occupy as much as 43% of the seats, spurring the election of increasing numbers of women at the district, provincial and national levels. Since the onset of PRI, the percentages of women in various levels of political activity have risen from 4-5% to 25-40%.

- According to Indian writer and activist Devaki Jain, *"the positive discrimination of PRI has initiated a momentum of change. Women's entry into local government in such large numbers, often more than the required 33.3 %, and their success in campaigning, including the defeat of male candidates, has shattered the myth that women are not interested in politics, and have no time to go to meetings or to undertake all the other work that is required in political party processes...PRI reminds us of a central truth: power is not something people give away. It has to be negotiated, and sometimes wrested from the powerful."*

Contrary to fears that the elected women would be rubber stamp leaders, the success stories that have arisen from PRI are impressive. A government-financed study, based on field work in 180 villages in the states of Uttar Pradesh, Rajasthan and Madhya Pradesh, and coordinated by the Center for Women's Development Studies in New Delhi, has found that a full two-thirds of elected women leaders are actively engaged in learning the ropes and exercising power. Says Noeleen Heyzer, executive director of UNIFEM, "This is one of the best innovations in grass-roots democracy in the world."

Women leaders in the Panchayati Raj are transforming local governance by sensitizing the State to issues of poverty, inequality and gender injustice. Through the PRI, they are tackling issues that had previously gone virtually unacknowledged, including water, alcohol abuse, education, health and domestic violence. According to Sudha Murali, UNICEF Communications Officer in Andhra Pradesh, women are seeing this power as a chance for a real change for them and for their children and are using it to demand basic facilities like primary schools and health care centres.

The PRI has also brought about significant transformations in the lives of women themselves, who have become empowered, and have gained self-confidence, political awareness and affirmation of their own identity. The panchayat villages have become political training grounds to women, many of them illiterate, who are now leaders in the village panchayats, Says Sudha Pillai, joint secretary in India's Ministry for Rural Development, "It has given something to people who were absolute nobodies and had no way of making it on their own. Power has become the source of their growth."

By asserting control over resources and officials and by challenging men, women are discovering a personal and collective power that was previously unimaginable. This includes women who are not themselves panchayat leaders, but who have been inspired by the work of their sisters; "We will not bear it," says one woman.

Once we acquire some position and power, we will fight it out...The fact that the Panchayats will have a minimum number of women [will be used] for mobilizing women at large." It is this critical mass of unified and empowered women which will push forward policies that enforce gender equity into the future.

An observation by Deepak Tiwari in This Week, India's No.1 Weekly News Magazine, displays the promising future made possible by the PRI. He notes,

> *"'Learning politics' is the latest fad for young village girls, who dream of joining the growing band of women panchayat representatives, 164,060 at last count, in the state."*

Statistical Summary

Social Indicator	India	World	Developing World	Kerala	Sri Lanka
Infant Mortality Rate, per 1000 live births	73	60	66	16	17
Maternal Mortality Rate, per 100,000 live births	570	430	470		140
Female Literacy, %	58	77.6	70.4	86.93	90.2
Female School Enrollment	47	62	57	63	67
Earned Income by females,%	26	58.0	53.0	49.8	35.5
Underweight Children, %	53	30	30		38
Total Fertility Rate	3.2	2.9	3.2	1.9	2.1
Women in Government, %	6	7	5		9
Contraception usage, %	44	56	54	56	66
Low birth weight babies, %	33	17	7		25

Kerala and Sri Lanka are added for comparison as they are recognized as having made exceptional efforts in the field of female education.

WOMEN IN PANCHAYATI RAJ

At the start of the new millennium, there are really two Indias. Together they comprise one-sixth of all humanity.

The first India-the modern India-has a remarkable record of accomplishment. Since independence in 1947, India has taken its place as a power on the global stage. It is the world's largest democracy and the 10th largest industrial power, with solid and consistent economic growth. It has the largest middle class of any nation, with the third largest scientific and technical workforce. Indian engineers hold top jobs in computer corporations on every continent. In agriculture, India is the number one producer in sugar, groundnuts (peanuts), tea and fruit. It is the number two producer in rice, wheat, vegetables and milk.

India's diverse and ancient religious traditions, its languages and its arts, are all part of its greatness. No nation has contributed more spiritual richness and truth to humanity. The list of winners of the major international prizes in literature, including the Nobel, Booker and Pulitzer Prizes, is filled with Indian writers and poets.

The second, and much larger, India is an entirely different world. Of the one billion people living in India today, 720 million-nearly three-quarters-live in rural areas characterised by grinding poverty and social injustice. This India has been bypassed by progress and opportunity.

At the dawn of the twenty-first century, most rural Indians live with the technology of a thousand years ago. In the age of the Internet, the majority cannot read and few have ever seen a computer. Living and voting in a democracy with constitutional guarantees, they remain powerless, locked in an oppressive system of economic exploitation, class division, caste prejudice and pervasive corruption. While the economy of modern India grows, the people lack access to education, nutrition and health care, sanitation, land and other assets that could enable them to escape the trap of poverty. Rural India has an infant mortality rate of 85, compared with 53 in the cities-and a life expectancy of only 54 years, compared with 63 in urban areas.

There is a truth that many would like to ignore: India's future will be determined in this "second India". Concern for the people of the second India is not merely humanitarian. Modern India has chosen to join the emerging global, information-based economy. To thrive in that economy, it must enter as one nation, with broadly based participation, productivity and prosperity. It cannot survive with rafts of wealth floating in a sea of poverty, and with the instability that comes with that condition. The nations that prosper in the global economy are those with a healthy and educated workforce, stable population growth and relative freedom from corruption and conflict.

India's recent history demonstrates that action from the top alone cannot meet the challenge. It will take the creativity, resources and participation of the entire population, many of whom have never before had a meaningful role or voice. For India, this means a two-fold revolution: the creation and nurturing of genuine participatory local democracy, and a profound transformation in the status and leadership of women.

In the critical areas for the well-being of the nation, women are on the "front lines". The future of rural India depends on overcoming enormous challenges in health, education, nutrition, population and environment. Women bear primary responsibility in every one of these areas-day after day after day. It is women who know best what needs to be done, and it is women who are most committed to taking those actions.

Yet, for thousands of years, India's rural women have been systematically denied the freedom, resources, information and decision-making power they need to carry out these responsibilities. In India, women have been kept in an almost unimaginable state of powerlessness, illiteracy, isolation and malnutrition.

India today faces an historic opportunity. As local democracy and expanded opportunity flourish around the world, India must not be left behind. The first step has been taken with the unprecedented 73rd amendment to India's constitution. This amendment mandates the transfer of decision-making power and resources in the rural areas to local democratic councils known as panchayats. Most revolutionary of all, one-third of all panchayat seats are to be reserved for women-guaranteeing them a role in determining the future of their communities. If fully implemented, women will, for the first time in India's history, have a voice in the decisions that affect their lives.

The struggle has only begun. Passage of the constitutional amendment on paper does not guarantee implementation in practice. Deeply entrenched interests oppose local democracy and women's rights, and are working to undermine this process directly and indirectly. There is a prevailing public cynicism regarding the possibility of grass-roots women's leadership. Removing these obstacles requires a social transformation of unprecedented proportions, demanding a concerted campaign lasting many years. The first generation of women panchayat leaders will need to possess enormous courage. Those supporting them will require great endurance.

The most strategic action that can be taken for India's future is to strengthen the hand of women panchayat leaders. The strategies and actions required to accomplish this are being shaped even now by an emerging network of committed individuals and organisations at all levels of society.

The transfer of power to one million women elected local representatives-many of whom are malnourished and illiterate-is the greatest social experiment of our time. These women are struggling against enormous odds to improve the lives of their families, their villages and their nation. They are the key change agents for a new future for India. By ensuring that they gain access to the resources and information they need-and by allowing their voices to be heard-India can finally become one nation. In doing so, it will fulfil its destiny and reveal its true greatness.

2

A Lifetime of Subjugation

If you want me to tell you what a nation is like... tell me the position of women in that country.

— *Jawaharlal Nehru*

A female in rural India faces some of the harshest discrimination in the world. Every phase of her life may be shaped by malnutrition, denial of selfhood and lack of voice in the decisions that affect her life.

The social and economic conditions that subjugate women are expressed and reinforced by the institution of dowry. To secure a husband for their daughter, a girl's parents must pay up to five times their annual income in dowry "gifts" to the husband's family. As a result, having a girl is a great burden, while having a boy is a great asset. Although dowry has been illegal since 1961, its practice is flourishing and on the rise, cutting across all classes and castes. For most women, there is no way out. Subjugation and submission are a pervasive pattern, enforced by violence and the threat of violence throughout their lives.

- *Unwanted before Birth.* Often, a baby girl in India is born into a family that had wished and prayed for a boy. Increasingly, girls are not born at all. Modern science allows parents to determine the sex of their child before birth-and abort it if it is a girl. In some areas, midwives or relatives simply murder the girl child-often considering it a "mercy killing". As a result, India now has a population ratio of 900 females (and in some areas as low as 600 females) to1,000 males.

- *Deprived as a Baby Girl.* Girls may be breast-fed for a shorter time than boys-in the hope that the mother can soon become pregnant with a boy. They are fed less food, and lower quality food. When girls become ill, they are less likely to receive medical care than boys-resulting in under-five mortality rates 43 per cent higher for girls than boys.
- *A Childhood of Drudgery.* By age five, girls carry adult responsibilities both inside and outside the home. At home, a girl cares for her younger siblings, and for her sick or pregnant mother. She fetches water, firewood and fodder, and makes dung cakes for fuel. Outside, she works in agriculture and wage labour. Thirty per cent of women's work burden in India is carried by girls between 6 and 11 years old. Education and play are nearly unthinkable.
- *Adolescence: Health Crisis and Sexual Violation.* Girls who reach puberty face a new set of harrowing and untreated problems of physical and mental health. At the very time her body needs more nutrition, she receives less. Adolescent girls suffer high rates of anaemia, vitamin deficiencies, tuberculosis, gynaecological problems, urinary tract infections and irregular menstruation. As almost everything in her life tells her she is worthless, her mental health deteriorates. Adolescent girls run high risks of sexual assault.
- *Marriage*: a new cycle of subjugation. She is married young, to an older man she has never met, and into a family and a village where she is a stranger. Early and frequent pregnancies about which she has little choice-and during which she rarely receives medical care-put her health at risk. She is isolated-often not permitted to leave the household, and thus unable to be assisted, supported or protected by other women.
- *Adulthood*: overworked and undernourished. A woman in India may work twice as many hours as her husband. Her triple burden-child-rearing, unpaid household work

and wage labour outside the home-goes unrecognised and unsupported. She is often malnourished throughout her life.

- *Outcast in Widowhood.* When her husband dies, a woman may be socially, economically and emotionally outcast, stripped of her only place in society. A widow in India is often forced to shave her head, eat only one meal per day and sleep on the floor.

THE CYCLE OF MALNUTRITION

The vicious cycle of malnutrition among the women of rural India perpetuates the equally vicious cycle of persistent hunger and poverty for all rural Indians.

India has the second worst rate of child malnutrition in the world, just behind Bangladesh. Low birth weight and child malnutrition are the primary determinants of ill-health and diminished capacity throughout life.

When children are born malnourished and underweight, they are at severe risk in all areas of personal development, health and mental capacity. They are physically weak and lack resistance to disease. They face a lifetime of disabilities, a lowered capacity for learning and diminished productivity.

The cost to India of this deficiency, solely in economic terms, has been estimated to be as much as US$28 billion per year in reduced GDP. This is greater than India's total annual public expenditures on nutrition and health combined.

This reality is a clear and direct result of the subjugation, marginalization and disempowerment of women throughout their lives.

We should not need to focus exclusively on women as mothers in order to be committed to transforming their status. Yet, in their role as mothers, they do represent the most critical link in the chain of human well-being and development.

It is widely recognised that the health and nutritional status of a pregnant woman dramatically affects the health of her baby. A more accurate scientific understanding, however, reveals that this is only part of the story. The truth is that a woman's health, from the time she is in her own mother's womb, is the single most important factor in determining the health of her child.

With this knowledge, it is clear that traditional responses to child malnutrition, such as simply providing nutritional supplements to pregnant women, are both inadequate and ultimately futile. If India is to interrupt the cycle of persistent hunger, the lifetime health and nutritional status of women must improve dramatically.

This, in turn, means transforming the way women are treated in the family and society as a whole:

- No longer can she eat last and least, taking whatever is left over after feeding the husband and sons.
- No longer can a girl-child be kept from the breast so that her mother may become pregnant sooner-to bear a son.
- No longer can teenage girls facing the stresses of puberty also expect to face deprivation, pregnancy and abuse.

WOMEN-INDIA'S INVISIBLE PRODUCERS

"...to fetch, to carry, to cook, to wash...year after year a submissive silent slave sold to life for nothing."
— from Silver Shackles by Maitrayee Mukhopadhyay

Rural India depends on its women for survival.

Its children and families are fed, clothed and sheltered by the labour of women. Its water and firewood are gathered by the hands of women. Its family farms and rural economy are productive because of women's work.

Yet, when men are asked, they say women do nothing at all. Because of women's low social status, their work goes unacknowledged, unvalued and unsupported.

Women carry a triple burden. They make indispensable contributions in all areas of rural life and economic activity, particularly in household maintenance, agriculture, and income-generating activities.

Household Maintenance

Women and girls have primary responsibility for all household work, and caring and providing for their families. They are traditionally responsible for collecting water, fuel and fodder (animal feed).

- Women hold full responsibility for cooking, cleaning and washing, and caring for children, the sick and the elderly.
- Women may cook for more than three hours per day with a biomass stove-burning wood, dung and crop residues. The smoke they inhale is equivalent to 20 packs of cigarettes per day. It causes eye and respiratory problems, bronchitis and lung cancer.

Agriculture

- Women contribute between 55 per cent and 80 per cent of total farm labour. Their work includes planting, transplanting, cultivation and weeding, watering, fertilising and harvesting.
- Women provide 50 per cent of the intensive labour in rice cultivation.
- Women account for 93 per cent of total employment in dairy production.
- In most households, women are responsible for all post-harvest processing and preservation.
- Women are generally not allowed to use agricultural implements. They perform many arduous tasks, such as transplantation and weeding, with their bare hands.

Income-generating activities

- Women are critical income earners for the family. They engage in small business ventures including silk cocoon rearing, vegetable oil extraction, spice preparation and fish farming.

- Women raise animals for milk, eggs, wool, leather and meat, as well as for use as draft animals.
- Women are involved in various paid labour activities, which are often severely physically taxing. Women's work includes cutting rocks and stones, construction, digging and carrying loads on their heads.
- Women constitute 51 per cent of total employment in forest-based small-scale enterprises such as basket, broom and rope making. Women who transport firewood on their heads may make two to three trips per day to the forest, carrying as much as 20-25 kilograms (44-55 pounds) of wood per trip.

Unequal Pay for Unequal Work

Despite their hard work, women are rarely compensated for their labours.

In a 1992 study of family-based textile workers, male children who helped in a home-based hand-loom mill were given pocket money, while the adult women and girls were not.

When women do earn an income, it is significantly less than men's. In the state of Tamil Nadu, women's agricultural wages are only 57 per cent of men's.

When women control their own income, they invest in the well-being of their children and families, while men often spend earnings on alcohol and leisure.

VIOLENCE AGAINST GIRLS AND WOMEN

"Violence against women and girls, many of whom are brutalised from cradle to grave simply because of their gender, is the most pervasive human rights violation in the world today.

"Long after slavery was abolished in most of the world, many societies still treat women like chattel: Their shackles are poor education, economic dependence, limited political power, limited access to fertility control, harsh social conventions and inequality in the eyes of

law. Violence is a key instrument used to keep these shackles on.

"Stopping violence against women and girls is not just a matter of punishing individual acts. The issue is changing the perception-so deep-seated it is often unconscious-that women are fundamentally of less value than men. It is only when women and girls gain their place as strong and equal members of society that violence against them will be viewed as a shocking aberration rather than an invisible norm." — Charlotte Bunch, Executive Director of the Centre for Women's Global Leadership, in UNICEF's The Progress of Nations, 1997

VIOLENCE AGAINST GIRL CHILDREN AND ADOLESCENTS

Feticide and Infanticide

- Between 3 million and 5 million female foetuses are aborted in India each year. In one Bombay clinic, 7,999 out of 8,000 aborted foetuses were female.
- Indian gender-detection clinic advertisements suggest that it is better to spend US$38 now to terminate a female foetus than US$3,800 later on her dowry.
- More than 10,000 girl children each year are killed when they are born. Girl children are murdered by suffocation, having their spines snapped, or having rock salt shoved down their throats.
- The Intentional deprivation of girl children-through insufficient breast-feeding and denial of food and health care-leads to malnutrition and death. This mistreatment, along with feticide and infanticide, has led to 50 million women "going missing" in India's population.

Rape and Sexual Abuse

- Sudhir Kakkar has estimated that at least 600,000 to 700,000 Indian children are likely to have experienced sexual abuse, most by members of their own families.

- For every crime reported against children, there are 100 that are not reported.
- The incidence of rape of girls under age 10 increased by 27 per cent between 1996 and 1997.
- 20 per cent of the pregnancies of adolescent abortion seekers in Mumbai were due to rape and incest.

Child Prostitution

- Between 70,000 and 100,000 prostitutes were working in the six major cities of Bangalore, Mumbai, Calcutta, Delhi, Hyderabad and Chennai in 1991.
- 15 per cent of Indian prostitutes are children.

Child Marriage

- 36 per cent of girls in rural India are married between ages 15 and 19, with percentages much higher in some states. In Rajasthan, 56 per cent of girls married before the age of 15. Of these, 3 per cent are less than five years old, and another 14 per cent are under age 10.
- Many girls have their first child while they are still teenagers. These young mothers face the stresses and risks of childbirth before their bodies have matured, and have a high incidence of maternal mortality.
- Young married girls have little control over when and how often they have children. 37 per cent of live births occur within two years of the previous birth. Infant mortality for these children is more than twice as frequent as it is for those more widely spaced.

VIOLENCE AGAINST WOMEN

Physical abuse and Domestic Violence

- In spite of the fact that most spousal abuse goes unreported, more than 70 per cent of women in some regions report physical abuse by their husbands.
- Wife-beating is often seen as "a husband's right". Divorce is not an option for battered wives.

- Alcohol abuse contributes to the likelihood that men will beat their wives.

Dowry Deaths

- As many as 15,000 women annually are killed by their husbands in disputes over dowry. Reported dowry deaths have increased by 170 per cent in the past decade.
- Thousands more are injured and maimed because the husband, or the husband's family, is dissatisfied with the dowry brought by the wife.

Psychological Abuse

- The United Nations Declaration on the Elimination of Violence Against Women cites psychological harm as a major form of violence against women.
- Women suffer from belittlement, threats, taunting and confinement. This can lead to depression and even suicide.

Violence in Motherhood

- India's maternal mortality rate-at 570 deaths per 100,000 live births-is among the highest in the world.
- Battered pregnant women are twice as likely to miscarry and four times as likely to have a low-birthweight baby.
- Children born to battered women are 40 times more likely to die before age five than children of non-battered mothers.

Abuse in Widowhood

- Widows in India are frequently harassed, beaten and even murdered.
- 15,000 widows are abandoned to temples where they have no protection from sexual violence.

Awakening to a New Possibility

The subjugation of women is ingrained in Indian society. It has been so much a part of ordinary reality that it is largely unseen, unexamined and unquestioned. Yet today, after thousands of years of silent acquiescence, the women of India are awakening to a new possibility--a future based on selfhood, equality and full participation. This awakening is part of a dramatic world-wide shift in consciousness about women and their role in society. A global struggle and a global stand. The twentieth century saw the roots of women's emancipation take hold in many parts of the world. One hundred years ago, in 1900, women had the right to vote in only one country--New Zealand. By the 1920s, women had won the vote in Great Britain, most of Europe and the United States.

In 1948, the year after India's independence, the United Nations adopted the Universal Declaration of Human Rights, proclaiming for the first time in history the "equal rights of men and women". In the years that followed, the struggle continued and took on momentum. In 1972, the United Nations General Assembly proclaimed that 1975 would be International Women's Year, launching an historic series of international conferences dedicated to the proposition that the world community will no longer tolerate the subjugation, marginalization and disempowerment of one-half of humanity.

Global women's conferences were held in Mexico City in 1975, in Copenhagen in 1980, in Nairobi in 1985 and in Beijing in 1995. Women's issues moved to the forefront of the international agenda in global conferences on food, environment, population and human rights.

The shift in India. India has a long history of women's activism, and Indian women have been leaders in the emerging global women's movement. It has only been in the last 10 years, however, that this shift in thinking has begun to be felt within Indian society itself.

There were some important precursors. Thanks to years of activism, India made dowry illegal in 1961. In the 1980s, the Indian government began to acknowledge women as key actors in development, instead of treating them only as welfare recipients. In 1985, it converted its Division for Women's Welfare into the Department of Women and Child Development.

Various states began to experiment with the reservation of seats for women in local political offices. Agitation began for a national-level reservation for women's participation at every level of the political system, resulting in one of the most important triumphs to date--the reservation of seats for women in panchayati raj. The most revolutionary step. The 1992 passage of the 73rd and 74th amendments enshrined the commitment to women in the constitution, reserving one-third of the seats in local self-government institutions for women. These reservations promise India's women--for the first time--real access to decision making power and resources.

Sisters, how much longer are you to keep silent? Now the time has come to open your mouth.--Pro-women slogan created at an Indian workshop:

> *Women's rights are human rights. Human rights are women's rights.— Rallying call for women's groups at 1993 World Conference on Human Rights in Vienna*

> *"The peoples of the United Nations have in the Charter reaffirmed their faith in fundamental human rights, in the dignity and worth of the human person and in the equal rights of men and women."*
> *— Universal Declaration of Human Rights, 1948*

> *"Discrimination against women violates the principles of equality of rights and respect for human dignity, is an obstacle to the participation of women, on equal terms with men, in the political, social, economic and cultural life of their countries, hampers the growth of the prosperity of society and the family, and makes more difficult the full development of the potentialities of women in the service of their countries and of humanity." — Convention on the Elimination of All Forms of Discrimination Against Women, 1979*

THE SHIFT IN WORLD CONSCIOUSNESS

1948: The Universal Declaration of Human Rights proclaims "the equal and inalienable rights of all members of the human family".

1975: The First United Nations Women's Conference in Mexico City establishes the women's movement as a global phenomenon, and launches the UN Decade for Women.

1979: The Convention on the Elimination of all forms of Discrimination Against Women (CEDAW) calls on nations "to modify the social and cultural patterns of conduct of men and women...which are based on the idea of inferiority or superiority of the sexes".

1980: The Second United Nations Women's Conference in Copenhagen first addresses the issue of women and development.

1985: The Third United Nations Women's Conference in Nairobi helps to catalyse the emergence of women's NGOs world-wide.

1992: India's parliament passes the 73rd and 74th amendments to the constitution, promising grass-roots democracy and radically new roles for women as leaders.

1993: Women's groups at the World Conference on Human Rights in Vienna declare that women's rights are human rights, and human rights are women's rights.

1993: The Declaration on the Elimination of Violence against Women proclaims that "violence against women constitutes a violation of the rights and fundamental freedoms of women".

1995: The Fourth World Conference on Women in Beijing calls for gender issues to be fully mainstreamed into government policies and actions--making women full and equal partners in society, and creating a strong platform for action and advocacy for women.

2000: Women mobilise in New York for Women

2000: Beijing +5, to hold governments accountable for the commitments they made at Beijing, and to powerfully include new issues of domestic violence in the platform for action.

3

Panchayati Raj: Local Democracy in Action

India is poor because the villages of India are poor. India will be rich if the villages of India are rich. Panchayats should be given greater power; for we want the villagers to have a greater measure of real swaraj [self-government] in their own villages.
— Jawaharlal Nehru, first Prime Minister of India

In spite of its status as the world's largest democracy, the vast majority of Indians, and particularly the 720 million people who live in rural villages, are largely dependent upon remote and unresponsive government structures historically characterised by bureaucracy, corruption and lack of transparency.

In many parts of rural India, there has been a deep rift between the people and their government. Rural people rarely receive information about the plans and actions of government. They lack ways to influence policies, programmes, or resource allocations for development. Many have no effective means of participating in shaping their future, and government officials are not always accountable to the communities they purport to serve.

It is no wonder that progress in improving the conditions of life in most parts of rural India has been slow to nonexistent.

As Nobel Prize-winning economist Amartya Sen has pointed out, "Democracy is not only the goal of development, it is the primary means of development". Only when every individual experiences greater freedom, voice and opportunity will each fully bring her or his creative powers to bear on solving the problems of the community.

The challenges facing rural India can never be solved by top-down, bureaucratic interventions. The critical needs of communities in health, sanitation, clean water, education, family planning and income can only be met locally-through local responsibility, accountability and action-utilising local resources to the greatest possible extent.

This truth, and the Gandhian principle of gram swaraj (village self-government), were recognised at the time of India's independence, but were not made a part of the constitution, never institutionalised and never fully put into practice.

Only in 1993, with the adoption of the 73rd amendment to the constitution, did India begin a process with the potential to create genuine democracy at the village level. It represents an historic opportunity to transform the face of rural India.

The 73rd amendment establishes panchayati raj: a system of local democracy through local councils known as panchayats. The amendment mandates that resources, responsibility and decision-making power be devolved from central government and placed in the hands of rural grass-roots people, with elections every five years.

The most revolutionary aspect of the amendment is that one-third of all panchayat seats are reserved for women. Rural women-who for centuries have lived in conditions of malnutrition, illiteracy and powerlessness-are now taking leadership roles in addressing these very issues.

This revolution is not going unopposed. Social and political elites in many areas are seeking to undermine and nullify panchayati raj, since they perceive it as a threat to their monopoly on power and a challenge to their domination of society. The democratic process is held back by an entrenched patriarchal and feudal mind-set that insists that panchayati raj-and certainly women's leadership-will never work. The forces that oppose local democracy are the same forces that hold the subjugation of women in place.

The destiny of the nation. For India to build a broad-based, solid foundation for economic and social progress, it must uproot the vestiges of feudalism and instil democratic values and practices. The people who live in India's 750,000 villages must become the authors of their own lives, and women must be respected and supported as equal partners in the process of development.

BASIC FACTS ABOUT PANCHAYATI RAJ

- *Tradition*: Panchayats are an ancient form of local government based on the idea that when five (panch) elders come together, God will be present.
- *Gram swaraj* (village self-government) was a goal of India's Freedom Movement, although it was not originally enshrined in India's 1951 constitution.
- Until the 1960s, panchayati raj served as the foundation for rural development in India's first two five-year plans. As bureaucratic power increased, panchayati raj was allowed to die in most states.
- The passage of the 73rd amendment in 1992 by the Indian parliament became part of the constitution in April 1993 after many years of national discussion and debate. The late prime minister, Rajiv Gandhi, championed the rebirth of panchayati raj.
- *State Action*. The amendment required every state to pass or amend its own panchayat act by April 1994, and to hold elections by April 1995.
- *A Three-tier System*. The amendment created a system of local democracy at the village level (gram panchayat), the block level (panchayat samity, the lowest level of the government bureaucracy, encompassing 10-20 panchayats), and the district level (zilla panchayat, comprising 4-10 blocks).
- *Gram Sabha*. To ensure that the panchayats themselves stay accountable to all the people of their constituency, they are required to hold village assemblies (gram sabha)

several times each year, with a quorum of citizens attending.

- *Reserved Seats*. The 73rd amendment reserves seats for the most powerless members of society on a revolving basis, as determined by the election commission. One-third of all seats-including one-third of all panchayat presidencies-are reserved for women. In addition, seats are also reserved for members of scheduled tribes and scheduled castes proportional to their population.
- *Devolution of Powers*: The "11th schedule" of the amendment specifies 29 areas of responsibility, covering all key aspects of village life, which states may transfer to the panchayats-along with sufficient resources and decision-making authority. In practice, most states have transferred very little power and few financial resources to the panchayats.

Panchayat responsibilities. The 11 schedule of the 73rd amendment specifies 29 areas of responsibility that states may devolve to the panchayats. *Note: areas marked in **bold** are areas where independent observers have indicated that women bear primary responsibility.*		
1. **Agriculture, including agricultural extension** 2. Land improvement, implementation of land reforms, land consolidation and soil conservation 3. **Minor irrigation, water management and watershed development** 4. **Animal husbandry, dairy and poultry** 5. **Fisheries** 6. **Social forestry and farm forestry** 7. **Minor forest produce** 8. Small scale industries, including food processing industries 9. Khadi (homespun cloth), village and cottage industries	• Rural housing • **Drinking water** • **Fuel and fodder** • Roads, culverts, bridges, ferries, waterways and other means of communication • Rural electrification, including distribution of electricity • Non-conventional energy sources • **Poverty alleviation programmes** • **Education including primary and secondary schools** • Technical training and vocational education • **Adult and non-formal education**	• Libraries • Cultural activities • Markets and fairs • **Health and sanitation, including hospitals, primary health centres and dispensaries** • **Family welfare** • **Women and child development** • **Social welfare, including welfare of the handicapped and mentally retarded** • Welfare of the weaker sections, and in particular, of the scheduled castes and the scheduled tribes • Public distribution system • **Maintenance of community assets**

WOMEN AS CHANGE AGENTS

The greatest social experiment. The historic confluence of forces taking shape in India-the awakening of women and the emerging commitment to local democracy-have led to what is unquestionably the greatest social experiment in the world today: the transfer of decision-making power to one million elected women local government representatives.

These women are not only the beneficiaries of change-they are the key agents for change.

Women and the Freedom Movement. Throughout India's long struggle for independence, women stood shoulder to shoulder with men. The Freedom Movement was their movement, and the battles were their battles. In fact, it was a woman-the Rani of Jhansi who fired the first shot that began the freedom struggle in 1857.

While the women of India worked, fought and died for freedom, few have been able to share the fruits of that freedom. They remain subjugated, marginalized and disenfranchised, as they have been throughout history.

Today, their struggle is again the nation's struggle. Freedom for India's women means freedom for India to create a new future.

Women face harsh opposition. The forces of patriarchy and feudalism that oppose local democracy also resist women's assumption of leadership roles in that democracy. Women who dare to contest and win local elections are often victims of manipulation, physical attack, violence and humiliation. A mind-set of cynicism pervades India-portraying elected women representatives as puppets of men. Yet, study after study has shown that once women come into power, the overwhelming majority exercise power independently.

Women are making a difference. Against all odds, women in panchayati raj are already making headway in areas of immediate concern to their families and their villages. These issues, often ignored by men, range from health and sanitation to campaigns against alcoholism and domestic violence. At the dawn of this new millennium, many of the entrenched social evils that have persisted for thousands of years are beginning to change.

Women are transforming the development agenda to address issues critical to village life:

- *Health*: Women-who are most often affected by poor health throughout their lives-take a stand for better nutrition, sanitation facilities, safe drinking water, and access to reproductive health care essential for healthy families and communities.
- *Education*: Women organise literacy courses for other women in the community. They ensure that schools are built for children, that teachers are held accountable, and that both girls and boys attend.
- *Income Generation*: Women form self-help groups and credit organisations among themselves to increase family income. Women leaders organise skills training for the women of the community.
- *Addressing Social Evils*: Women take action to address crucial social issues such as dowry, domestic violence, child marriage and child labour. They ensure that women know their rights and have access to information. They commit themselves to include traditionally excluded groups-the landless, scheduled castes and tribes.
- *Redefining Leadership*: Women are changing the nature of leadership, incorporating values such as honesty, openness, patience, collective support, inclusion and accountability.
- *Changing Village Dynamics*: In even the most conservative villages, women's leadership unleashes a process of change for the whole community. Women leaders empower other women to step out of the home, become literate and contribute to the community. They help to dissolve old prejudices, creating new partnerships with men.

The Case of Kerala

While the state of Kerala falls below India's average in terms of traditional economic measures, it has been a pioneer in both implementing panchayati raj and investing in women. For the past three decades, it has focused heavily on education, land reform and health services-especially for young mothers. It has a strong panchayat system, and has devolved significantly more responsibility and resources to its panchayats than have other states. This commitment has paid off in dramatic and lasting improvements in quality of life for its rural people.

Even with the second highest population density, and a per capita income that is below the national average, Kerala has achieved a female literacy rate of 82 per cent-one of the highest in all of Asia. It has a life expectancy of 74 years-15 years above the all-India average-and the lowest death rate for every age group among all Indian states. Most significantly, Kerala's infant mortality rate stands at an impressive 17, compared with 83 for the nation as a whole. This means that for Kerala, hunger can be said to have ended as a society-wide issue.

AGENDA FOR ACTION

There are two major prerequisites to broad-based progress in rural India:

- Panchayats must become effectively responsible for all key areas of village life.
- Women must be empowered as key leaders in the panchayats.

Achieving these goals will require a sustained multisectoral campaign of action, producing breakthroughs in each of the following priority areas:

Panchayats

Reserved Seats: Panchayats and people's organisations must ensure that representatives serving in seats reserved for women, as well as for scheduled castes and tribes, are actively supported in attending meetings and engaging in panchayat activities.

Training: All panchayat members must gain access to the training they need to carry out their responsibilities in all key areas, including panchayat finance, nutrition and health, family planning, sanitation, education and economic development.

Gender Sensitisation: Male panchayat members and government officials must have the opportunity, through workshops and training programmes, to appreciate and become more sensitive to the importance of women's leadership and the challenges women face.

Women Representatives

Leadership Training: Leadership training and ongoing support must be available for the development of the leadership skills women need and want-the ability to create a vision, to speak and listen powerfully, to build constituencies and to make things happen.

Literacy Training: Women panchayat leaders who cannot read when they are elected (as many as 50 per cent in some states) must have access to literacy training.

Networking: Women representatives must have the opportunity to share experiences, learn lessons, and build structures of mutual support that enable them to experience themselves as part of a state, national and international network of women travelling the same path.

Government

Elections: Ensure that panchayat elections are held every five years.

Devolution of Authority and Responsibility: Establish legislation at the state level that effectively transfers all 29 areas of responsibility to the panchayats, particularly those related to women.

Transfer of Resources: Ensure that adequate finances are allocated to panchayats to carry out their work, and are delivered for use in a timely manner, without undue restriction or delay.

Political Will: Government leaders at the national and state levels must express leadership and act consistently in support of panchayati raj and devolution of power to the local level.

Bureaucratic Support: Officers at the national, state and district administration levels must work actively with panchayats, facilitating their access to resources and removing obstacles to their progress.

Access to Information: Rural people-and particularly women-must gain access to all information about the responsibilities and entitlements of panchayats. All relevant legislation, regulations and budget documents must be readily available and translated into local languages, along with straightforward information on the many government programmes to which the rural poor are entitled.

Judicial Activism: The judicial system must provide prompt and firm support for the full implementation of panchayati raj.

Avoidance of Parallel Structures: Government ministries must channel decentralisation strategies through the panchayats rather than creating alternative or parallel structures.

Alliances for Advocacy and Action

Alliance Building: NGOs, women's groups and other civil society organisations must form vibrant and active networks and alliances dedicated to advocacy and co-ordinated, strategic action for panchayati raj and women's leadership in the panchayats.

Public Awareness: These alliances must create a climate of awareness and support for panchayati raj throughout all sectors of society.

Communication and Information Flow: The alliances must facilitate effective and open communication between the government and panchayats to ensure that information about available resources, programmes and initiatives are available and fully understood.

A National and International Spotlight: The alliances must keep the efforts of the panchayats and women representatives visible and present on the state, national and international agendas.

Media

Education and Political Awareness: Media must provide thorough and ongoing coverage of the historic process of building local democracy, with particular emphasis on the rarely told story of women's successes as panchayat leaders.

Accountability: Through its ongoing scrutiny and reporting, the media need to keep a spotlight on the actions of government officials in the implementation of panchayati raj.

THE PANCHAYATI RAJ CAMPAIGN

The Hunger Project in India is committing itself to ignite and sustain a co-ordinated, strategic campaign of action for women's leadership and the success of panchayati raj.

The Hunger Project is beginning this initiative in four states where there has been strong official support for panchayati raj: Gujarat, Karnataka, Madhya Pradesh and Rajasthan. It intends to expand the campaign to all 11 states where The Hunger Project works.

Four-pronged Strategy: The Hunger Project's Panchayati Raj Campaign initially has four major components: alliance-building, leadership training, increasing media coverage and generating international support. The Hunger Project will identify additional high-leverage pathways for action as the campaign unfolds.

1. *Building Alliances for Advocacy and Action*: Women's leadership and panchayati raj are opportunities of such scale and importance that such a campaign can only be carried out by an alliance of organisations in each state committed to this issue. The Hunger Project is working strategically to build strong and active alliances among government agencies, NGOs, self-help groups, academics and media in support of women's leadership in panchayati raj.

2. *Leadership Skills Training*: India is blessed with many organisations providing training to equip women panchayat leaders with key factual information, such as the roles and responsibilities of panchayats, and details of government programmes. What appears to be missing-and what The Hunger Project is in a unique position to provide-is training for these women in fundamental leadership skills.

   Elected women representatives have grown up in an environment that tells them, day after day, that they-as women-are powerless. They have had precious few opportunities to develop their leadership skills. The Hunger Project has created a new Women's Leadership Workshop to enable women to have a breakthrough in their leadership skills, and to empower their leadership over time.

   Vision, Commitment and Action: In the workshop, women discover that they possess the power to actually change conditions they have considered both intolerable and hopeless. They generate their own vision for what they want to achieve, and learn how to inspire others to stand with them to achieve it. After a lifetime of doing only what they have been told, women discover their ability to create their own strategies and action plans. In the months following the training, participants come back together to support each other in achieving their goals.

3. *Increasing and Improving Media Coverage*: The Hunger Project has held workshops and press conferences to educate reporters about the untold success stories of women in panchayati raj. To enhance and expand this effort, The Hunger Project is launching the Sarojini Naidu Prize for Best Reporting on Women in Panchayati Raj.

4. *International Support*: India's pioneering work in panchayati raj sets an important example for countries around the world. People in both developed and

developing countries need to know about and maintain support for these efforts. Through strategic communications and site visits, The Hunger Project is mobilising its global constituency to put and keep the international spotlight on this historic phenomenon.

THE SAROJINI NAIDU PRIZE

For Best Reporting of Women in Panchayati Raj

Sarojini Naidu (1879-1949) was a poet of repute and an orator and was popularly known as the "Nightingale of India". A close associate of Mahatma Gandhi, she was a prominent leader of the freedom movement and was president of the Indian National Congress in 1925. After independence, she became the first woman governor of an Indian state.

The press plays a critical role in India. Throughout the twentieth century, India's media have participated in the Freedom Movement, generated response to famine and disaster, and strengthened Indian democracy. India's new constitutional commitment to women's leadership in panchayati raj is the next unfolding of human freedom and development in India.

It is time for the press to make another important contribution. Only through accurate and increased coverage of the historic process of women's participation in panchayati raj-including their battles to achieve hard-won successes-can the mind-set of cynicism be broken and the conspiracy to undermine panchayati raj be halted. Given the critical role of the press in this historic process, The Hunger Project is committed to supporting and encouraging the press to energetically and prominently report the breakthroughs and success stories of women's leadership in panchayati raj.

The Sarojini Naidu Prize will annually honour three journalists for outstanding reporting on women in panchayati raj. The awards will be presented in each of three categories:

- Best Hindi-Language Reporting
- Best English-Language Reporting
- Best Reporting in other languages

Cash Award: Each prize will include a Rs 2 lakhs cash award to enable the reporter to continue his or her work on this issue.

October 2: In recognition of the importance placed by Mahatma Gandhi on panchayati raj and the full participation of women in public life, the award will be presented on Mahatma Gandhi's birthday each year in New Delhi, beginning on 2 October 2001.

CHANGE AGENTS FOR A NEW FUTURE

Across India, The Hunger Project is seizing the historic opportunity of the election of one million grassroots women to local government. As women take office, they shift the agenda towards health, education, nutrition and family income. The Hunger Project has a four-prong strategy to empower these women leaders:

- Leadership Training for women representatives
- Making panchayats effective through mobilizing people's participation and advocacy to shift resources and authority to the local level.
- Alliance Building to support these women in achieving their vision
- Mobilizing the media to transform public attitudes
- LATEST NEWS: April 2007: THP-India Update to the Global Board
- March 6, 2007-Hunger Project plays leadership role in national celebration of International Women's Day

A COMPARISON BY STATE

The concept "status of women" eludes precise definition and hence precise measurement. Status can be perceived in different ways: the extent of a woman's access to social and material resources within the family, community and society (Dixon, 1978), or her authority or power within the family/ community and the prestige commanded from those other members (Mukerjee, 1975), or her position in the social system distinguishable from, yet related to, other positions (Committee on the Status of Women in India, 1974), or the extent to which women have access to knowledge, economic resources and political power as well as the degree of autonomy they have in decision-making and making personal choices at crucial points in their life-cycle (United Nations, 1975). The idea of status also connotes the notion of equality (Krishnaraj, 1986). There can be self-perceived status, group-perceived status or objective status (Mukerjee, 1975), a situation which can lead to status inconsistency when a person is very high in one type of status and very low in another.

Women's Status in Retrospect

During the Vedic and Rigvedic periods (approximately 4000-1000 BC), women in India held equal status with that of men (Kuppuswamy 1975; Choudhury, 1978). The degradation of women started only since 300 BC. The patriarchal joint-family system, structure of property ownership, early marriage, self-immolation of widows (sati) or state of permanent widowhood, all became obstacles to the development of women (Neera Desai, quoted in Kuppuswamy, 1975:243). Since the late nineteenth and early twentieth centuries of the common era, several reformers fought against those aspects of the system that have resulted in the oppression of females. To them, women should labour under no dissatisfaction not suffered by man, and as a result of their efforts, independent India has adopted several rules and regulations to protect the rights of women and establish equality of status.

India is home to a diverse group of people characterized by different languages, customs, traditions, religions, life-styles or habits. Virtually each State has its own culture, which is very important in studying any aspect of this society (Davis, 1973) including the status of its women.

Objectives and Indicators

Three types of comparison are attempted in this paper: (a) an inter-state comparison of the status of women, (b) an intra-state comparison of the status of women vis-a-vis that of men in each State, and (c) a comparison of status of women in relation to overall development.

This analysis of the objective status of women (as perceived by others on the basis of the outward manifestations of some selected characteristics) uses secondary data. Fourteen States having a population of 10 million or more are considered in the study, which together accounted for 313 million females in 1981 and 379 million in 1991. Some generally accepted proxies for "status" are identified and used within the constraints of data availability. Indicators such as a woman's control over resources and the laws of inheritance governing her right to property, perhaps would have reflected female status better, but could not be included because of the non-availability of data.

In all, 28 variables are considered; they reflect the status dimensions of education, employment, health, demographic situation and overall development. Owing to data limitations, the study relates to the early 1980s since most of the pertinent information is available only for that period rather than the current decade. However, this situation should not be of much concern in assessing a slowly changing society like India where drastic social changes normally do not occur in the short span of 10 years.

A list of the selected variables and the abbreviations by which they will be referred to in the text of this paper is provided below:

No.	Description of variables	Abbreviation
1	Percentage of female enrolment in classes I-V to the population in the 6-10 year age group	PSE
2	Percentage of female enrolment in classes VI-VIII to the population in the 11-13 year age group	MSE
3	Percentage of female enrolment in classes IX-XII to the population in the 14-17 year age group	HSE
4	Percentage of female enrolment in colleges for general education to the population in the 18-23 year age group	CE
5	Literacy rate in the 10-29 year age group	LR
6	Percentage of the female population with graduate or higher level of education in the 20-24 year age group	PG

Contd...

No.	Description of variables	Abbreviation
7	Percentage of the female population (60 years and above) educated to the level of matriculation and above to the total population of older persons	OEP
8	Percentage of female paid workers in the 20-39 year age group to total population of workers in the same age group	APW
9	Percentage of females working in the modern sector	MSW
10	Percentage of female elected officials per 100,000 workers	EO
11	Infant mortality rate	IMR
12	Expectation of life at birth	ELB
13	Total fertility rate	TFR
14	Percentage of ever-married girls aged 10-19 years	EMG
15	Singulate mean age at marriage	SMAM
16	Urban population as a percentage of the total population	PUP
17	Net irrigated area as a percentage of the net cropped area	PNIA
18	Electricity consumption per capita (kwh)	ECPC
19	Total road length per 100 km2	TRL
20	Motor vehicles per 10,000 population	MV
21	Daily newspaper circulation per 1,000 population	DNPC
22	Percentage contribution of the manufacturing sector to the total gross domestic product	PCMS
23	Per capita income at 1970/71 prices	PCY
24	Percentage of the population below the poverty line	PBPL
25	Number of beds per 1,000 population	BPTP
26	Percentage of births attended by trained professional	PIB
27	Government expenditure on health as a percentage of total government expenditure	GEH
28	Percentage of villages electrified	PVE

Variables 1-7 represent the situation with regard to education; variables 8-10 are employment indicators; 11-12 health indicators; and 13-15 demographic indicators relevant to female status. The remaining variables (16-28) indicate various aspects of overall development.

Education

In order to create a sense of community among men and women at home and at work as fellow and equal human beings capable of playing many roles--many of them shared and interchangeable--women must be educated and allowed to participate in all activities (OECD, 1975).

In India, the roles traditionally assigned for men and women are that of bread-winners and home-makers, respectively. Thus, the education of girls is not seen as an important requirement for preparing girls for their future role as "home-makers". As such, in States where, besides economic need, the social and individual demand for education is also recognized, one would expect a higher rate of enrolment of girls in schools and a higher proportion of educated women in the population than is actually the case. In reality, women's creative and intellectual potentials are either ignored or underplayed in education in India. As a consequence, generally fewer women are found to have had the opportunity of gaining a higher level of education in India. This pattern of behaviour cannot be attributed to current attitudes alone; they have been molded over several generations. This particular aspect is represented by the percentage of educated older persons in each State.

Employment

Remunerative employment is considered to be one of the major status-deciding factors. The common belief is that man's high status within the family is due to his position as bread-winner. It is argued that, if a woman's economic dependence can be reduced by her ability to earn an income outside the household, she would enjoy a higher status, which would be the case if there was not much difference in the nature of the work done by males and females (Lal, 1979).

In this study, employment is represented by adult paid workers, modern sector workers and elected officials. Women's participation in paid employment has been found to be highly related to their status (Safilios-Rothschild, 1986 and 1990), because it shows the tendency among women to earn a living or to augment the family's income by working for others. Women's participation in modern sector work is a step ahead of any other type of paid employment. The modern sector is defined in this paper as including all professional, technical, administrative, executive, managerial, clerical and similar work. Until recently, some of these occupations have been monopolized by males. Consideration of the indicator "elected officials" helps to show the extent of female participation in overall decision-making from the panchayat (village council) to the central Government levels.

Health

Infant mortality rate and expectation of life at birth are accepted indicators of the health situation of any population. In societies where there is no discrimination between the sexes, women, on average, survive for a longer period than men (Sinha, 1983). In view of this situation, female mortality should be either less than or equal to that of males. Where this is not the case, it can be argued that women do not receive adequate attention (reflecting low status), which leads to higher female mortality rates.2/ Other things remaining equal, higher mortality of women would indicate low status compared with States where female mortality is lower.

Women, Marriage and Fertility

Marriage is practically universal in India and large families seem to be the norm even today after more than 40 years of implementing a family planning programme. Early marriage of girls, although illegal, is an accepted practice in many parts of the country. The majority of girls and women in India are infant not allowed by their parents to decide on either the age at which they would like to get married or their partners. This indicates that, in societies where a large segment of the population are poor and where the age at marriage is low, parents are transferring the burden of feeding their female children to someone else as soon as they possibly can (Dandekar, 1974).

Thus, it may be concluded that the status of females is comparatively lower in India than in societies where females marry at an older age. The singulate mean age at marriage and the proportion of ever-married girls in the 10-19 year age group are two of the three indicators used in this regard. The total fertility rates has been selected as the third indicator under the assumption that a high TFR indicates little control by women over their fertility behaviour owing to their low status.

Overall Development

The development indicators 16-28 are used to determine whether the differences in status, if any, are reflections of differences in the levels of overall development. The various development aspects covered here are urbanization, agriculture, manufacturing, electricity consumption, transport and communication, health and economic situation. In all, 13 variables are included.

Methodology

All the States studied are ranked on the basis of each of the selected indicators: the better the situation is, the higher is their rank. These ranks are examined below to determine status differences; however, it is possible that the same State may not be ranked uniformly high or low for all the chosen indicators.

Hence, we use a taxonomic method to rank States on the basis of different dimensions of status. The taxonomic method, which was designed by a group of Polish mathematicians in 1952, enables the determination of homogeneous units in an n-dimensional space without having to employ statistical tools such as regression, variance and correlation.

The method, although lengthy, is comparatively more lucid and simple than the other types; central to its use is the concept of average value. We chose this method because it is suited for ranking, comparing and classifying regions of a country by levels of development, standard of living, status or any other such aspect. (For a detailed description of the method, see Harbinson and others, 1970; Reddy, 1977.) Briefly stated, the steps involved in this method are given below:

(a) A set of n points representing states 1,2,3,...,n for a group of indicators 1,2,3...,m are arranged in a matrix form;

(b) Since the aim of the method is to construct a single index, it is necessary to add the values of the $\frac{Xij - \bar{X}j}{Sj}$ indicators at some stage of the computation. Thus, in order to eliminate the influence of the different units of measurement, the indicator values are standardized using the following formula:

where

i =1,2,3,...,n;

j =1,2,3,...,m;

$\bar{X}j$ = mean of the jth indicator; and

Sj = standard deviation of the jth indicator.

A new matrix can be formed using the standardized values.

(c) The "distance" or difference from each state to every other state (1,2,3...,n) for each of the standardized values of the selected indicators is obtained by simple subtraction, with the results being arranged in matrix form.

(d) These several distances from the n-dimensional space have to be converted into a single mathematical expression with which states can be compared. The following formula can be used for this purpose:

$$Cab = \sqrt{\sum_{k=1}^{m} (Dak - Dbk)^2}$$

where

Caa = O;

Cab = Cba;.....; and

Cab ≤ Cak + Ckb

This will result in a symmetric matrix known as the distance matrix.

(e) The next step is to determine the graphical relationship (which has not been attempted in our study).

(f) A model or ideal state is then created with the best standardized values of the status indicators and the composite distance from this state to every other state in the matrix is calculated. The ranking of the differences from the ideal state is called the pattern of development and is obtained by using the following formula:

$$\text{Cio} = \sqrt{\sum_{k=1}^{m}(\text{Dik} - \text{Dok})^2}$$

where

Cio is the pattern of development;

i = 1,2,3,...,n and 0 is the best standardized value as determined from the matrix of standardized values [Step (b)].

FINDINGS AND DISCUSSION

Inter-State Comparison of the Status of Indian Women

For the comparison, States are ranked on the basis of each indicator value separately and also on the basis of a combined status index obtained by using the taxonomic method for each dimension.

Table 1 presents the results for education and employment; table 2, health and demographic indicators. Even though women's status is the subject under investigation in this section, male status ranks are also given in the tables to facilitate comparison of the pattern of status ranks between the two gender groups.

Table 1: Ranks of States on the basis of educational indicators

State	PSE(1)		MSE(2)		HSE(3)		CE(4)		LR(5)		PG(6)		OEP(7)	
	M	F	M	F	M	F	M	F	M	F	M	F	M	F
Andhra Pradesh	3	7	3	6	2	5	13	12	1	5	4	3	5	5
Bihar	5	3	1	1	1	1	11	2	2	2	2	1	7	4
Gujarat	12	10	8	9	11	11	3	7	11	10	11	10	10	9
Haryana	4	5	11	8	5	6	7	9	10	7	8	13	6	7
Karnataka	8	8	6	7	7	8	12	10	8	8	6	7	8	10
Kerala	11	14	14	14	14	14	10	14	14	14	1	9	9	14
Madhya Pradesh	6	4	5	3	3	4	4	4	4	4	7	6	2	2
Maharashtra	13	11	10	11	12	12	5	8	13	12	12	12	13	13
Orissa	7	6	2	5	4	7	8	3	6	6	3	2	1	1
Punjab	9	12	12	13	9	10	9	13	9	13	10	14	11	8
Rajasthan	2	1	4	2	8	3	6	1	3	1	9	4	3	3
Tamil Nadu	14	13	13	12	13	9	2	5	12	11	13	5	12	11
Uttar Pradesh	1	2	9	4	6	2	14	11	5	3	14	8	4	6
West Bengal	10	9	7	10	10	13	1	6	7	9	5	11	14	12

Notes: For an explanation of abbreviated indicator names, see pages 60-62 of text; M= male and F= female; in parentheses are the reference numbers of the variables provided in the list of variables on pp. 60-62.

Table 2: Ranks of states on the basis of employment, health and demographic indicators

State	Employment						Health				Demographic		
	APW(8)		MSW(9)		EO(10)		IMR(11)		ELB(12)		TFR (13)	EMG (14)	SMAM (15)
	M	F	M	F	M	F	M	F	M	F	F	F	F
Andhra Pradesh	3	1	2	1	9	5	9	11	7	10	9	5	4
Bihar	4	5	5	5	12	9	5	4	5	4	2	3	3
Gujarat	5	4	3	12	10	13	4	5	6	8	6	11	11
Haryana	10	13	12	13	2	2	10	6	12	9	5	6	6
Karnataka	12	8	8	4	14	11	13	13	11	12	11	9	9
Kerala	2	9	1	9	13	14	14	14	14	14	14	13	14
Madhya Pradesh	9	3	1	2	6	6	1	2	2	2	3	2	2
Maharashtra	14	10	13	11	11	12	11	12	10	11	12	10	7
Orissa	6	2	14	3	8	1	3	3	3	3	7	7	8
Punjab	1	14	6	14	1	10	12	10	13	13	10	14	13
Rajasthan	8	6	11	8	7	7	6	7	4	5	4	1	1
Tamil Nadu	13	11	9	6	4	3	8	8	9	7	13	12	12
Uttar Pradesh	7	7	4	10	3	4	2	1	1	1	1	4	5
West Bengal	11	12	7	7	5	8	7	9	8	6	8	8	10

Notes: Regarding abbreviations, see the list of variables.

Education

Table 1 shows the ranks of the States based on the seven educational status indicators (1-7). As can be seen from the table, there is no consistency with respect to all the variables in any State, although Kerala, Punjab and Maharashtra generally rank high, whereas Rajasthan, Orissa, Madhya Pradesh and Bihar rank low.

Employment

The ranks of the three indicators of employment (8-10) in table 2 show that, for Nos. 8 and 9 Punjab stands out with the highest rank for women whereas Andhra Pradesh has the lowest rank. Other states with high ranks are Haryana, West Bengal and Tamil Nadu for No. 8 and Haryana, Gujarat and Maharashtra for No. 9. In addition to Andhra Pradesh, on the lower side are Orissa, Madhya Pradesh and Gujarat for No. 8 and Madhya Pradesh, Orissa and Karnataka for No. 9. The situation with respect to No. 10 is slightly different, in which case Kerala, Gujarat, Maharashtra and Punjab rank high and Orissa, Haryana, Tamil Nadu and Uttar Pradesh rank low.

Health

Ranks based on the two health variables show that Kerala has the highest rank for both No. 11 and No. 12; the ranks are more or less the same for both the indicators in all the States (table 2). Uttar Pradesh has the lowest rank for the health status of women followed by Madhya Pradesh, Orissa and Bihar in that order.

Demographic Situation

Table 2 also provides values for Nos. 13-15 in an attempt to determine how fertility, marital status and age at marriage reflect on inter-State variations in female status. Because these indicators are fertility related, status ranking is restricted to females only. The result shows that Rajasthan has the lowest rank followed by Bihar, Madhya Pradesh and Uttar Pradesh in that order. Kerala has the highest rank followed by Tamil Nadu, Punjab and Karnataka, respectively.

Intra-State Comparison of Women's Status vis-a-vis that of Men's

Because a variable-by-variable gender comparison would be very cumbersome to perform, a combined status measure was calculated with the help of the taxonomic method to represent the variables for each dimension of status (the results are presented in the Appendix). The status measure shows that, except for a few cases such as Kerala, Punjab, Karnataka and Maharashtra for health; Kerala for female education; Maharashtra and Karnataka for male employment; and Punjab for female employment, the measures indicate low status for both males and females in all States. Table 3 ranks the States on the basis of this status measure. The ranking of States based on the educational index, which reflects overall educational development, shows Bihar to be the lowest in terms of educational status for women. It is followed by Rajasthan, Orissa, Madhya Pradesh and Uttar Pradesh in that order. By contrast, Kerala, Punjab, Maharashtra and West Bengal show higher educational status for women.

Table 3: Ranks of States on the basis of different dimensions of status

State	Education		Employment		Health		Total*	
	M	F	M	F	M	F	M	F
Andhra Pradesh	4	6	5	1	7	10	2	6
Bihar	1	1	9	7	5	4	3	2
Gujarat	10	10	7	11	4	6	8	10
Haryana	7	7	6	10	10	7	10	7
Karnataka	8	8	13	9	12	12	11	9
Kerala	14	14	2	12	14	14	7	14
Madhya Pradesh	2	4	11	3	2	2	4	3
Maharashtra	13	12	14	13	11	11	14	12
Orissa	5	3	4	2	3	3	5	1
Punjab	11	13	1	14	13	13	9	13

Contd...

State	Education		Employment		Health		Total*	
	M	F	M	F	M	F	M	F
Rajasthan	3	2	10	5	6	5	6	4
Tamil Nadu	12	9	8	4	9	9	13	8
Uttar Pradesh	6	5	3	6	1	1	1	5
West Bengal	9	11	12	8	8	8	12	11

Note: * = Combining all educational, employment and health variables.

Table 4: Male-female difference in status measure for education, employment and health indicators

State	Education	Employment	Health	Total*
Andhra Pradesh	0.1459	-0.2777	0.1138	0.1540
Bihar	0.0062	-0.1386	-0.0904	0.0443
Gujarat	0.0688	0.1249	0.0468	0.1505
Haryana	0.0451	0.1486	-0.1958	0.0303
Karnataka	0.0695	-0.3725	-0.0529	0.0611
Kerala	0.2513	0.3277	0.0000	0.5070
Madhya Pradesh	0.0923	-0.3044	0.0542	0.0379
Maharashtra	0.0471	-0.2962	-0.0224	0.0077
Orissa	0.0442	-0.2317	0.0253	-0.0116
Punjab	0.1697	0.6994	-0.0998	0.3040
Rajasthan	0.0061	-0.1706	0.0138	-0.0091
Tamil Nadu	-0.0316	-0.1225	-0.0353	-0.0115
Uttar Pradesh	0.0622	0.0550	-0.0574	0.1148
West Bengal	0.1178	-0.1622	-0.0245	0.0759

Note: * = Combined for all educational, employment and health variables.

The differences in gender status, which can be determined by a comparison of the ranks given in the table, show that five States, namely Bihar, Gujarat, Haryana, Karnataka and Kerala, have the same rank for both male and female educational status. In Andhra Pradesh, Madhya Pradesh, Punjab and

West Bengal, female status ranks are better than that of males even though the difference is not very significant. In Maharashtra, Orissa, Rajasthan, Tamil Nadu and Uttar Pradesh, males have higher ranks which indicate better status, although the rank differences are negligible.

Status rank differences between males and females are higher in the case of employment than in health or education. Also see table 2 where the status rank is quite high for females compared with males in Punjab and Kerala, and quite low in Madhya Pradesh for variable No. 8. As for variable No. 9, wide differences are noticeable, i.e. Gujarat, Kerala, Punjab and Uttar Pradesh show a high rank for females whereas Orissa shows a noticeably low rank. In the case of variable No. 10, there is a wide gap in the rank of States, with Orissa favouring males and Punjab favouring females.

It seems that males are favoured with regard to employment status in nine States: Andhra Pradesh, Bihar, Karnataka, Madhya Pradesh, Maharashtra, Orissa, Rajasthan, Tamil Nadu and West Bengal; females are favoured in the remaining five States: Gujarat, Haryana, Kerala, Punjab and Uttar Pradesh.

In terms of health status, a comparison of the ranking of males shows that their status is not much different from that of women, since nine out of the 14 States show the same rank for both sexes. Wide variations in ranks can be observed in Kerala and Punjab, where female status is comparatively higher than that of males. Similarly, in Madhya Pradesh the difference between males and females is quite wide, with males being favoured. The relevant information for comparing status according to gender is shown in table 4. The values in this table have been obtained by subtracting the values for female status from that of males. Thus, an equal status, whether high or low, will give a zero value. Similarly, the larger the difference is between the values, the higher is the status difference, a positive sign indicating better female status and a negative sign indicates the opposite.

Interestingly, the differences obtained are negligible in most cases, particularly so in terms of health and education.

Thus, one may be tempted to conclude that, with respect to these two dimensions, the status of males and females is more or less the same. There are few exceptions: the health and educational status of females is comparatively high in Andhra Pradesh, and in Haryana, male health status is high; in Kerala, Andhra Pradesh, Punjab and West Bengal, female educational status is better.

Employment status differences, according to gender, are quite noticeable. Of the 14 States, males enjoy better employment status in all States, except for Gujarat, Haryana, Kerala, Punjab and Uttar Pradesh. In the case of Uttar Pradesh, the difference is not as noticeable as in the case of the others. The maximum difference in employment status is in Punjab where it favours females. Similarly, a fairly noticeable difference favouring females can be observed in Kerala also.

The last column of table 4 represents the total of all three dimensions. The differences are negligible, expect for Andhra Pradesh, Gujarat, Kerala, Punjab and Uttar Pradesh, all of which favour females. The difference is exceptionally high in the case of Kerala, with Punjab following not far behind.

The close relationship between male and female status within the States in terms of health and education, and the lack of such a relationship in terms of employment are further substantiated by the rank correlations calculated for each variable and presented below:

	Variable No.	Rank correlation coefficient	Variable No.	Rank correlation coefficient
Education	1	0.8769	2	0.8374
	3	0.8066	4	0.4725
	5	0.8769	6	0.4022
	7	0.8725	Total	0.9277
Employment	8	0.2835	9	0.1035
	10	0.5912	Total	-0.0374
Health	11	0.9253	12	0.9253
	Total	0.9473		

The male-female status ranking is highly correlated with health and education, except for higher-level education where the relationship is comparatively weak. As for employment, except for variable No. 10, the other rankings show almost no relationship at all.

Women's Status and Development

Table 5: Ranks of States based on selected overall development indicators circa 1981

State	PUP (16)	PNIA (17)	ECPC (18)	TRL (19)	MV (20)	DNPC (21)	PCMS (22)	PCY (23)	PBPL (24)	BPTP (25)	PIB (26)	GEH (27)	PVE (28)	Total
Andhra Pradesh	8	9	8	5	4	6	3	8	7	6	8	9	8	6
Bihar	2	10	1	6	2	2	7	1	1	2	3	5	1	2
Gujarat	12	7	12	3	11	11	11	11	12	10	10	1	9	10
Haryana	7	13	13	8	10	1	8	13	13	7	14	4	13	9
Karnataka	11	3	9	9	12	8	12	9	8	8	9	2	7	8
Kerala	4	2	5	14	9	14	9	7	11	14	13	13	13	12
Madhya Pradesh	5	4	6	2	6	4	6	3	2	1	5	8	2	3
Maharashtra	14	1	11	4	13	13	14	12	9	13	7	6	10	13
Orissa	1	6	4	11	1	3	1	2	4	4	2	11	5	1
Punjab	10	14	14	12	14	9	5	14	14	12	12	7	13	14
Rajasthan	6	5	3	1	5	7	2	5	10	5	1	14	6	4
Tamil Nadu	13	11	10	13	8	10	13	6	5	9	11	12	11	11
Uttar Pradesh	3	12	2	7	3	5	4	4	3	3	4	3	3	5
West Bengal	9	8	7	10	7	12	10	10	6	11	6	10	4	7

Notes: The totals provided in the last column are based on the index developed with the help of the taxonomic method; regarding abbreviations, see pp. 60-62.

Table 6: Ranks of States based on the combined measure of different dimensions of status and overall development

State	Development	Education, employment and health		Demographic
		Male	Female	
Bihar	1	5	1	7
Orissa	2	3	2	2
Madhya Pradesh	3	4	3	3
Rajasthan	4	6	4	1
Uttar Pradesh	5	1	5	4

Contd...

State	Development	Education, employment and health		Demographic
		Male	Female	
Andhra Pradesh	6	2	6	6
Karnataka	7	11	9	11
West Bengal	8	12	11	8
Haryana	9	10	7	5
Tamil Nadu	10	13	8	13
Kerala	11	7	14	14
Gujarat	12	8	10	10
Maharashtra	13	14	12	9
Punjab	14	9	13	12

As stated previously, 13 indicators were selected for development and their rankings are given in table 5. With the help of the taxonomic method, a combined development measure has been computed. It produced a value for most States that was above 0.6, indicating that actually no State is well developed in terms of the variables selected. The lowest value of the development measure is 0.4184 for Punjab, indicating that it is comparatively better developed than the others, although Maharashtra, Kerala, Tamil Nadu and Gujarat have fairly high values too. Orissa seems to be the least developed State; others with low levels of development are Bihar, Madhya Pradesh, Rajasthan and Uttar Pradesh.

Table 6 gives the status ranking of the States based on the combined variables of education, employment and health, demographic situation, and overall development. The table shows that in six out of the 14 States, the ranks of the total female status measure and that of development are the same; however, it is of particular importance here to note that they are all at the lower level. Orissa is at the lowest rank for both women's status and development. Similarly, other States with the same ranks for both status and development (Bihar, Madhya Pradesh, Rajasthan, Uttar Pradesh and Andhra Pradesh) are all at the lower level of development also. States that rank higher in development and lower in women's status are Gujarat, Haryana, Maharashtra, Punjab and Tamil Nadu. States which rank high in women's status and low in development are Karnataka, Kerala and West Bengal. The results of the rank correlation between the ranks of development and that of the status dimensions are as follows:

Sex	Health	Education	Employment	Demographic development
Male	0.6923	0.8769	-0.0374	-
Female	0.7319	0.9121	0.7980	0.7846

Except for male employment, the coefficients are quite high and positive, thus indicating a fairly high and direct relationship between status and development.

Conclusion

It may be clearly observed from this study that the efforts made by the Government of India for over four decades to bring women into the mainstream of society are slowly paying off as the status indicators are found to have more or less the same ranking for both males and females in many States. But some States, such Orissa, Madhya Pradesh, Bihar and Uttar Pradesh, have been found to be at a low level with respect to health, employment and educational status. They also have the same low status ranks with respect to overall development. These findings point to the direct relationship between status and development; many of the (objective) status indicators are reflections of overall development. Hence, these States need special attention in order to raise them up to the level of the other States in terms of development.

One important question that arises from this study is: Is women's status a phenomenon to be studied at the macro level using macro-level data? If the answer is yes, the lack of significant differences between the status of males and females either reflects on the choice of indicators (though often used elsewhere for status measurement), or indicates that there are only negligible status differences between males and females in many States of India, unlike what is generally believed to be the case. We suspect that this conclusion is not correct because of the observed direct relationship between ranks of development and status, which indicates perhaps that what are read as status differences are nothing more than differences in levels of development. This confusion can be overcome only by making in-depth studies focusing more on the perceptions of men and women about their own status and comparing the results with the results of macro-level analyses. In the final analysis, status is a personal, innate experience of an individual resulting from his or her life situation and that of others acting upon and reacting to each other. As such, it is a multi-dimensional phenomenon, which, in essence, should be handled very carefully in order to derive any meaningful conclusion.

Measures of status according to education, employment, health, demographic aspects and development, by State

State	Education		Employment		Health		Total*		Demo-graphic	Develop-ment
	M	F	M	F	M	F	M	F	M	F
Andhra Pradesh	0.8558	0.7099	0.6896	0.9673	0.5155	0.4017	0.9084	0.7544	0.5972	0.7551
Bihar	0.8877	0.8815	0.5332	0.6718	0.6291	0.7195	0.8990	0.8466	0.8391	0.9100
Gujarat	0.6319	0.5631	0.6094	0.4845	0.6338	0.5870	0.7248	0.5743	0.3663	0.5722
Haryana	0.7085	0.6634	0.6719	0.5233	0.3470	0.5428	0.6708	0.6405	0.6190	0.6078
Karnataka	0.6908	0.6213	0.2255	0.5980	0.2841	0.3370	0.6582	0.5971	0.3384	0.6381
Kerala	0.4205	0.1692	0.7730	0.4453	0.0000	0.0000	0.7559	0.2489	0.0000	0.5686
Madhya Pradesh	0.8759	0.7836	0.4956	0.8000	0.8544	0.8002	0.8585	0.8206	0.7993	0.8665
Maharashtra	0.5342	0.4871	0.1427	0.4389	0.3445	0.3669	0.4832	0.4755	0.3699	0.5356
Orissa	0.8423	0.7981	0.7151	0.9468	0.7892	0.7639	0.8445	0.8561	0.4270	0.9060
Punjab	0.5983	0.4286	0.9900	0.2906	0.2277	0.3275	0.7061	0.4021	0.2331	0.4184
Rajasthan	0.8692	0.8631	0.5099	0.6805	0.6216	0.6078	0.8086	0.8177	0.8567	0.8488
Tamil Nadu	0.5370	0.5686	0.5775	0.7000	0.4455	0.4808	0.5941	0.6056	0.1992	0.5695
Uttar Pradesh	0.8042	0.7420	0.7330	0.6780	0.9134	0.9708	0.9223	0.8075	0.7798	0.8404
West Bengal	0.6514	0.5339	0.4613	0.6235	0.4934	0.5179	0.6475	0.5716	0.3968	0.6735

Note: * Combining all education, employment and health variables.

4

GANDHI AND STATUS OF WOMEN

WOMEN'S STATUS AT THE TIME

When Gandhiji assumed India's leadership the average life span of an Indian woman was only twenty seven years. Babies and the pregnant women ran a high risk of dying young. Child marriage was very common and widows were in very large number.

Only 2% of the women had any kind of education and women did not have an identity of their own. In North India, they practiced the purdah (veil) system. Women could not go out of the house unless accompanied by men and the face covered with cloth. The fortunate ones who could go to school had to commute in covered carts (tangas).

It is in this context that we have to recognize the miracle of Gandhi's work. Gandhiji claimed that a woman is completely equal to a man and practiced it in strict sense. Thousands and millions of women, educated and illiterate, house wives and widows, students and elderly participated in the India's freedom movement because his influence.

For Gandhiji, the freedom fight was not political alone; it was also an economic and social reform of a national proportion. After a couple of decades, this equality became very natural in India. After India's freedom (in1947) and adoption of constitution (1950), emphasized equality of women, when Hindu code was formulated, the population was not even impressed. They said- "Of course, it had to be done."

WOMAN AND PROGRESS

Gandhiji always advocated a complete reform which he called "Sarvodaya" meaning comprehensive progress. He believed that the difference between men and women was only physical and has expressed several times in his writings that in many matters especially those of tolerance, patience, and sacrifice the Indian woman is superior to the male. You will discover this when you read his articles from "Young India" and "Harijan".

During the 40 years of his political career, he only found more reasons to deepen his faith in what he wrote. He never had a specific program for women, but women had a integral role to play in all his programs. I feel that this is one of the reasons why women participated in his programs so overwhelmingly.

Gandhiji declared that there is no school better than home and there is no teacher better than parents. He said men and women are equal, but not identical. "Intellectually, mentally, and spiritually, woman is equivalent to a male and she can participate in every activity."

Indian society is a male dominated one. Gandhiji has illustrated in his autobiography (The stories of my experiments with truth) how early in his marriage he too wanted to dominate his wife. He often said that paternal society is the root cause of inequality. In his book, there is a very touching chapter about when he asked his wife to clean a public toilet and the resulting conflict between him and his wife. He has written how ashamed he was of himself, and how he took care not to hurt her anymore for the rest of his life. Even though there was big gap between him and his wife intellectually, it did not affect their family life. He has said that Kasturba followed her husband more than was expected of her.

Gandhiji followed Bramacharya (strict discipline of food, drinks, and of celibacy) from a very young age, but when his wife passed away, Gandhi grieved that without Ba, his life would have been meaningless. That was the bondage of his 62 years of marriage.

WOMAN AND SOCIAL SERVICE

Gandhiji struggled very hard to understand a woman's physical and mental pain. From a young age he introduced his wife and children to social sacrifice and service. He believed that service has to be performed for self-fulfillment, not for public consumption or exhibition. He believed that the publicity given to one's social service actually decrements the value of the service. He tried very hard to eliminate job indignity and bias based on caste system. He tried to do the work of a barber, dhobi (washer man), and janitor to understand them and demonstrate that the work one does has no impact on one's status in the society.

For me, the fact that he contributed a great deal in raising his children is very modern concept. On one occasion the white midwife would not show up for his wife's delivery and Gandhiji himself delivered his child. He helped wife with feeding, bathing, and toiletries of the infant. In western countries these days men are encouraged to be with their wives during the delivery and the men are supposed to pitch in with diaper changing, etc. Gandhiji practiced this very modern concept 90 years ago in his own family.

ROLE OF WOMEN

"Womanhood is not restricted to the kitchen", he opined and felt that "Only when the woman is liberated from the slavery of the kitchen, that her true spirit may be discovered". It does not mean that women should not cook, but only that household responsibilities be shared among men, women and children. He wanted women to outgrow the traditional responsibilities and participate in the affairs of nation. He criticized Indian's passion for male progeny. He said that as long as we don't consider girls as natural as our boys our nation will be in a dark eclipse.

Child Widows

Gandhiji was especially considerate of the young widows. In the last 80 years, as a nation, if we have made any progress on the matter of child widows (girls used get married very early and after untimely deaths of their husbands, they were condemned to a life of great agony, shaving heads, living in isolation, and shunned by the society.) it is due to the reformers like Gandhiji and his contemporaries. Gandhiji once noted during his legendary travels across India that he never came across 13 year old who was not married. He declared the marriages in which the girls were not consulted were unholy. At that time in Madras presidency, the number of child widows were alarmingly large. He called upon the young to marry the widows and also to boycott child marriages. (It may be noted here that Gandhiji himself married when very young; he was thirteen.) The history of India knows of many such young men who married widows and went on to work as social reformers.

Temple Women and Prostitutes

Gandhiji was very disturbed by the plight of this low caste untouchable section of the society, namely the Devadasis. He was hurt by the miserable way the children of brothels were treated. He had made elaborate plans for their rehabilitation. He declared that protecting women's honor was important and as holy as protecting cows. His book "Women and Social Injustice" contains discussions of very deep thoughts and solutions on the topic. He felt that after India became free, the system of temple women and brothels must be abolished. Even though on paper we have abolished the system of Devadasis, rampant exploitation of women as sex servants has continued. There was no way Gandhiji could have predicted modern ways and means of prostitution (call girls, phone sex etc) but he certainly identified its social evil and tried to fight it.

Gandhiji's Contribution for Betterment of Women in India

As we look back at the Indian history and compare the conditions of women before Gandhi's rise, and now, the progress we have made is quite enormous. A whole generation of women leaders came up influenced by Gandhi's vision. If today in India so many women can go to work in offices, educational institutions, and factories without fear or hesitation, the roots for such system were laid 90 years ago by Gandhiji and his followers.

As mentioned earlier, Gandhiji formulated India's freedom struggle as a comprehensive plan for women's development. Even though a lot of inequalities remain in our society, there is a fundamental agreement that men and women are equal. As Indians, we can be very proud that the same cannot be claimed even by so called "advanced nations". In Britain as well as in the U.S.A., women could not vote 75 years ago. But women's voting came very naturally to us from the beginning. About 100 years ago, the western woman could not own property, get a divorce or take the custody of her children. We just have to look at the life and struggles of Dr. Annie Besant to understand the status of western women during Gandhiji's time. The western women had to take to streets, overcome many stereotypes to establish themselves voting and other rights. But for us, political, economic and voting rights came so naturally through the constitution!

Legacy

Today, if Gandhi's agenda has fallen apart, it is due to Indian politics. The continued exploitation of women can be attributed to the degradation in moral values of the society, and utter poverty of our nation. We ignored the role of social service, job dignity, and self reliance. Once in a while we run into true volunteers who believe in Gandhiji's ideals and have implemented his programs. I hope that at least a few of the younger generation take up Gandhiji's unfinished manifesto and work to eliminate social barriers facing women.

A Synopsis by India

- Contrary to sensational reports sometimes appearing in the news-hungry media in both India and other countries, female infanticide, bride burning (for reasons of dowry) and 'sati' (widow burning) are NOT normal in India. Each of these acts is a criminal act and an extremely rare occurrence.

- Enron Corporation's (Power Division) CEO Rebecca Mark, a woman, has inadvertently highlighted that women are taken at a par with men in government and business. She managed to rescue a contract her company had won but had run into trouble with a state government in India.
- India has the world's largest number of professionally qualified women.
- India has more female doctors, surgeons, scientists and professors than the United States.
- India has more working women than any other country in the world. This includes female workers at all levels of skill-from the surgeon and the airline pilot to bus conductors and menial labourers.
- On an average however, women in India are socially, politically and economically weaker than men.
- Moves are underway to empower women. The most news-making development was the introduction of the Women's Bill in Parliament in late 1998: the Bill seeks to reserve a certain percentage of seats in Parliament for women. This Bill is most likely to be passed by Parliament in 1999.
- There is a National Human Rights Commission for Women that handles all human rights violations against women. There is a National Council for Women that advocates policy for Women. There is an entire ministry for women that formulates and implements policy for them.

OTHER ABUSES FOR WOMEN IN INDIA

The problem of drug use and addiction among women cannot be separated from other aspects of their social existence and conditioning. The social and economic status of women directly impinges on their freedom in real terms. Their status is therefore of great relevance in cases of substance abuse by women themselves, and even more so where women suffer the consequences of such abuse by members of their family.

Women in India: How Free? How Equal?

India ranks 115 in the Human Development Index of 2001 (UNDP, 2001). The country has made considerable progress since independence; economic reform and liberalization measures over the 1990s have led to strong economic growth, increased exports and reduced inflation. Overall life expectancy is 62.9 years, and projections for 2000-2005 suggest that life expectancy of males and

females will be 63.6 years and 64.9 years respectively (United Nations Population Division, 2000). According to the 2001 Census, overall literacy has increased to 65.38 percent (Census of India, 2001).

What does this mean for the country's women?

A report commissioned by the United Nations Resident Co-ordinator in India (Menon-Sen and Shivakumar, 2001) titled 'Women in India: How Free? How Equal?' raises several disturbing issues concerning the current status of women in India. The study's main findings are outlined below. Data from the Census of India 2001 and the Human Development Report 2001 also corroborate some of the study's observations.

These Include: Although the absolute number of females has grown 21.79 percent in the last decade, the male-female ratio is still lower than it was 100 years ago. In societies where men and women are treated equally, women tend to outlive and outnumber men. Typically, one would expect to find 103-A report commissioned by the United Nations raises several issues concerning thecurrent status of women in India.

The 2001 Census reveals an adverse ratio of 93 women for every 100 men. With the exception of Kerala, every state has fewer women than men. India, in the words of Amartya Sen, has to account for some 25 million 'missing women'.

The Indian girl child is disadvantaged right from birth. The sex ratio for girl children between the age of 0 and 6 years is 927, strengthening the fear that some girl children are never born or have no opportunity to survive.

Only 54 percent of women are literate as compared to 76 percent of men.

More than 36 percent of the population lives below the poverty line. Many of them are women.

There are far fewer women in the paid workforce than there are men.

In some states such as West Bengal, Orissa, Bihar, Assam and Arunachal Pradesh, between 63 and 85 percent of married women suffer from anaemia (IIPS, 2000 and ORC Macro 2000).

The average Indian woman bears her first child before she is 22 years and has little control over her own fertility and reproductive health.

In 1998-1999, only 48 percent of married women in the reproductive age group used any form of contraception (World Population Monitoring, 2000). This figure is much lower (30%) in poorer states like Uttar Pradesh and Bihar.

For many women, abortion is the only method of contraception available.

More than 570 women die per 100,000 births (World Population Monitoring, 2000), 70 percent due to totally avoidable reasons.

Women are under-represented in governance and decision-making positions.

Most women do not have any autonomy in decision making in their personal lives.

In Madhya Pradesh and Rajasthan, less than 50 percent of women have access to money in thc houschold (IIPS and ORC Macro, 2000).

Women face violence inside and outside their family, as well as at the workplace. The impact of drug use on women, both directly and indirectly, needs to be understood within the context of these realities.

Police records for the country as a whole show that a woman is molested every 26 minutes. A rape occurs every

34 minutes. Every 42 minutes, an incident of sexual harassment takes place. A woman is kidnapped every 43 minutes. And every 93 minutes, a woman is killed.

Contrasts between Women and Men in India

About 1/3 of the households are run by women alone because the men left the women to work in the city. And by the way, when a man and a woman have the same job, the woman gets much less money than the man. One thing that is important, too is that 2/3 of the women in India can't read and write, but on the contrary 2/3 of the men can read and write!

In the evening some women are not allowed to sleep before their husband or other men in the household. Unlike the women the men can leave their wife.

Burning Brides

In India sometimes women are burned if their parents didn't pay enough dowry when the girl got married. This is often called a"kitchen accident", in 99% of these "kitchen accidents" a woman is murdered. 4000 women are burned every year

Indian Widows

If a husband dies, his widow is always guilty, even if the man was a few years older. If the widow hasn't got a son, the indian people think that the widow must die, too, because they are useless. As a widow she isn't allowed to wear jewellery and the red circle on their forehead is called the "Bindi". The red painting is called the "Sindoor". The "Mangrustra" is a golden bracelett, it's like the wedding ring in europe. And, last but not least, the "Sati" this is when the women are burned when they are still alive.

The Marriage

The girls in India get married early. The parents of the girls want to get rid of them, so they start looking for a husband when she's at the age of 8 years. They get married so early, because if they pass the teen ages it's difficult to get them married. And one other reason is that the marriage costs much money. At the day of the marrige, most of the women see their husbands for the first time. When they get married the women have to promise to obey their husbands and take care of the parents in law. The main aim of the marriage is to get many sons because that is a blessing but getting many daughters is just like a curse. Many of the women are widowed early or they are singles because of their husbands who have deserted them.

Unintentional Daughters

The best gift in a marriage is to get many sons and no daughters, because in India people think that daughters bring bad luck and the parents of the girl are worried because they have to pay a high dowry to the parents in law when their daughter gets married. If the wife doesn't get any babys, the husband can leave his wife. One important thing is that the people don't have contraception or sex education like in Europe! They also have contraception like condoms and pills, but if a woman gets any pills from the doctor often the man uses them because he thinks that the pills are useless on a woman. Also if a woman is pregnant and she knows that the baby will be a daughter many have an abortion.

Statistics about Women in India

Here you can see a diagramm about the life expectancy in India and Germany. The life expectancy of women in India is much less than in Germany. In India most women die before the men.

WOMEN IN INDIA: ARE THEY BETTER OFF?

Nomination of three Indian elite class girls for Ms. World titles cannot cover the misery that more than 80% of the women go through every day in India.

The National Commission for Women (NCW) in India has recently released a report on rapes in India, titled as, 'Rape-A legal study.' It is a significant step in the wake of recent spurt in the incidents of rapes throughout India. Though the Report deals with the problem of rape in India, the authors also express their concern about the overall status of women in our society.

They seem to have arrived at the following conclusion in the Prologue of the Report itself, "in India, in ancient times, women had enjoyed an able position in the household and in society. As the 'queen' of the household, her position was envied by her counterparts elsewhere. Unfortunately, constant invasions by foreign elements from about 8th century changed the scenario to the detriment of women. Her vulnerability to abuse by the invading hordes bestowed upon man a responsibility to protect her and from thence developed the inherent dominant role of the male within the family fold and her inevitable dependence on the male. Long years of invasion and infliction of crime on her resulted in many protective measures. The direct effect of this state of affairs was perforce, keeping women within the four corners of the home and consequential enforced illiteracy which has been, by and large, her lot since then."

Unfortunately, this kind of thesis is not only over-simplification of a very serious issue of perpetual injustice being done to women not only in India but throughout the world but also means running away from finding a way out to stop atrocities against women. Is it not true that society like Chinese or Japanese, which were never subjugated, don't have a better record to show historically, so far as, the gender equality is concerned? In our case, long before the arrival of the 'invaders' in 8th century, women like Darupadis were not only put on bet but also disrobed publicly by the kinfolk.

We had kings like Ravan who enjoyed kidnapping helpless and pious women like Sita, and innumerable other good kings in our mythological epics maintaining 'harems' with innumerable wives. Shri Shiv Mahapuran not only equated women with death, degeneration, snake, poison and destructive fire but also concluded, "there is no bigger sinner than women. Women are the roots of sin, you must know." (Umasanhita, chapter 24)

The story of historical injustices to women in India or elsewhere is yet to have a pause, and is, too complicated to be wished away to some invaders' misdeeds only. It is true that Arabs and later Mughals who came to our lands from the western route in no respect believed in gender equality. It really was a matter of great irony and shame that these followers of Islam which normatively promised basic human rights to women more than 14 hundred years back were practitioners of a rigid patriarchal Islam. However, it is also true that the denigration of women has been a universal and perpetual phenomenon. The plight of women transcended the geographical, religious, cultural, ideological and civilizational barriers. It is true that before the advent of agriculture women enjoyed a better status but with the rise of feudal society they were gradually turned into serfs or objects of pleasure. The four Vedas are a great testimony of this changing scenario.

It is high time that organizations like NCW instead of wasting time on futile and questionable theses take a serious note of highly objectionable popular religious literature debasing women being circulated these days by organizations like Geeta Press, Gorakhpur and others. This kind of literature is easily available in every nook and corner of the country including the government allotted stalls at all major railway stations both in Hindi and English. Geeta Press publishes mass religious literature espousing the 'Hindu way of life' for women with titles like, 'How to Lead a Household Life,' 'Nari Shiksha,' and 'Striyon Ke Liye Kratawya Shiksha'. They have a bulky edition even preaching Sati. In the following are some of the samples from this literature.

"What should the wife do if her husband beats her and troubles her?" the answer is, "the wife should think that she is paying her debt of her previous life and thus her sins are being destroyed and she is becoming pure." "Is Sati pratha (viz. The tradition of wife being cremated with the dead body of the husband on the funeral pyre) proper or improper?" The answer to this query provided in one of these books reads, "a wife's cremation with the dead body of her husband on the funeral pyre is not a tradition. She in whose mind truth and enthusiasm come, burns even without fire and she does not suffer any pain while she burns. This is not a tradition that she should do so, but this is her truth, righteousness and faith in scriptural decorum." A Hindu woman must commit suicide because, "a Sati woman snatches her husband from the hands of Yamdoot and takes him to Swarglok (paradise)." This stream of literature openly decries equal rights between men and women, working women, co-education and upholds purdah.

Interestingly, Muslim clergy does not lag behind inpouring out this kind of anti-women literature for Muslim women in India. The 'Islamic' literature which is in circulation makes horrible reading and is available in many regional languages. Some of these books are titled as 'Musalman Biwi' and 'Mian Biwi Ke Haqooq'. One of these books even has a chapter, 'Right to Batter Wife' which reads, "husband may use the stick to beat the wife but he should avoid hitting her on the face or cause deep scar." The authors of such literature quote scriptures after scriptures to convey the message that a woman must treat her husband as master and herself as slave.

Those of you who think that "Dahi Bahlay and Kababs from Delhi are better than the ones from Karachi", please pay attention to what is happening here and assess whether the status of women in India is something to be proud of or not. Nomination of three Indian elite class girls for Ms. World titles cannot cover the misery that more than 80% of the women go through every day in India. Think about it.....!!!

EMPOWERING WOMEN

The last five decades have witnessed some basic changes in the status and role of women in our society. Today this process has been further accelerated with some women becoming increasingly self-conscious of their discrimination in several areas of the family and public life. They are also in a position to mobilise themselves on issues which affect them vitally, and constitute a significant segment in the electoral politics of the nation. Inspite of all these efforts, it is revealed that during the past decades the sex ratio in the country has been continually worsening.

Promoting Awareness

A large number of women are either ill-equipped or not in a position to propel themselves out of their traditionally unsatisfactory socio-economic conditions. They are poor, uneducated and insufficiently trained. Some tend to be ill-nourished anaemic and burdened by domestic chores and child care responsibilities. They are often absorbed in the struggle to sustain the family physically and emotionally and as a rule are discouraged from even taking an interest in affairs outside the home. There is an urgent need to encourage them to face the problems of illiteracy, lack of information and lack of skills, and try to find solutions to these problems.They should be made aware of their shortcomings in terms of education, nutrition and health.

There are many issues that require to be taken up for betterment of women in India. The recently announced national population policy is built on the correct premise that population stabilisation is a matter of human development. It is also important to look at this in the broader context of women's health and enhancement of their capabilities. Success will depend upon a number of related factors including simultaneous improvements in education, child health care, how effectively women get empowered to gain access to education, to make the right choices, and to influence decisions.

Education

Education of women is a critical input for improving nutrition levels, raising the age at marriage, acceptance of family planning, improvement in self-image, and their empowerment. In India female literacy rate is as low as 39.42 per cent as compared to 63.86 per cent of men. The need of the hour is to improve female literacy. With the exception of Kerala where the female literacy is 86.9 per cent, in the states like Bihar, Rajasthan, Uttar Pradesh and Madhya Pradesh less than 30 per cent women are literate. The recent UNDP report placed India 103 out of 174 in the rank of 'gender-related development index'. Education is the key to development. For educational development of women, a vigorous drive for universalisation of elementary education, retention of girl child in school, reduction in drop out rate and promotion of adult literacy was taken up by Government in the Five-Year Plans. Some of the special initiatives were, review of school text books to remove gender bias, re-orientation of school teachers to present gender equality and setting up of Women's Development Centre in Universities and colleges to bring about social awareness on women's issues.

Education is the basic tool for empowering a woman. This is where the NGOs and Social Service Sector people need to work. There are phases of empowerment. Once a girl undergoes the first phase of information, education and communication she becomes aware of her surroundings. Then comes the phase of accountability, where she is given the ability to rationalise and take informed decisions for which she is accountable. Once she is educated and empowered, she is in a better position to take care of herself and this needs to be sustained.

On one side where there is a need to educate girls, it is also necessary that the other sex be sensitised towards her. Cultural patterns tend to impose male superiority by assigning males with the roles of producers and heirs. It is important to usher in changes in societal attitudes and perceptions with regard to the role of women in different spheres of life. Adjustments have to be made in traditional gender specific performance of tasks. Mass media and inter-personal communication techniques should be utilised to achieve these ends.

Health Care

Equal status of women is difficult, as women are physically smaller in size and strength as compared to their male counterparts. To make woman physically healthy and may be able to take challenges of equality, she needs special health care and diet. NGOs/Social Service Sector people should look into this aspect and help the women to be enlightened about this. To be useful to the family, community and the society, they must take care of their own health. They must not only think of their husbands, children and in-laws but also think of themselves.

The seventies brought women to the forefront of development concerns. This happened with publication of the report of the committee on Status of Women in India, the observance of the International Women's year in 1975, preparation of a National Plan of Action for women and introduction of the Medical Termination of Pregnancy Act 1971.

Thirty years have gone by and a look at indicators of Maternal & Child Health (MCH) care, shows the poor current status of health of women. India like other South East Asian countries has a very high maternal mortality rate of 4.6 per 1,000 live births, Bangladesh 6, Nepal 8.3 where as USA 0.08 and Switzerland 0.05. Magnitude of the problem of anemia for pregnant women in South East Asian countries is high – 60 per cent in India, 77 per cent in Bangladesh and 68 per cent in Nepal in comparison to 29 per cent in America and 20 per cent in Europe. The sex ratio in India was 1,000 males to 978 females in 1901, which has come down to 1000 males to 927 females in 1991. Where as in developed countries like USA, Canada and Britain the ratio is 1000 males to 1080 females. How is it that the population of females in India is going down? Ultra sound, Amniocentesis to detect the sex of the foetus is followed by female foeticide. Besides other causes, female foeticide is one of the main causes for decrease in female population in India.

A girl is discriminated from the very childhood. At birth she is unwanted, she is not sent to school, she is given less food to avoid her to grow fast. After sad experiences of childhood in a woman's life come three phases that could be remembered with 3 Ms. These are – Menarche, Motherhood and Menopause.

At Menarche, she should be educated to take high protein diet and food items containing iron. She must also be educated about sexuality, teenage pregnancy (17 per cent of pregnancies are in age group of 15-18 years) complications of abortions. The next phase is motherhood. It is also important that she is aware about the do's and don'ts of pregnancy. Access to good health facility for check ups, extra diet rich in protein, calcium and iron, and the power to decide as to how many children she should have. Maternal Care Indicators show that only 62.3 per cent of pregnant women receive antenatal check ups, 53.8 per cent doses of Tetanus Toxoid, 50.5 per cent iron/folic acid tablets, and only 25.5 per cent deliver with propers health care facilities.

Lastly comes the phase of Menopause, when a woman reaches the age of 45 and generally stops menstruating. If she has an understanding of menopause and an understanding partner/husband and family, she gets over this phase smoothly. With the physical changes in this phase comes the need for self-respect and feeling of being wanted. Many a time family members are unable to show these in their behaviour.

The discrepancy in the ideology and practice of the empowerment policy of women in India constitutes its continued social, economic and cultural backwardness. As empowerment of women in a society is the most effective index of measuring modernisation and development, it should be ensured therefore that at every phase of life, a woman needs to be given special inputs in terms of school education, higher education, health education, sex education, population education and education on self development, so that these may improve her status in the society and better the quality of her life.

5

FEMINISM IN INDIA

INTRODUCTION

The history of feminism in India for the most part has been "The History of Doing" with a sparse theoretical writing in feminism. Pre-colonial social structures and women's role in them reveal feminism was theorized differently in India than west. Colonial essentialization of "Indian culture" and reconstruction of Indian womanhood as epitome of that culture through social reform movements resulted in political theorization (nationalism) rather than feminism alone.

DEFINING FEMINISM IN INDIAN CONTEXT

Historical circumstances and values in India make women's issues different from the western feminist rhetoric. 1) The idea of women as "powerful" is accommodated into patriarchal culture through religion. This has retained visibility in all sections of society; by providing women with traditional "cultural spaces" 2) in west the notion of "self" rests in competitive individualism emerging from "born free yet chained every where" as compared to India where individual is just one part of the larger social collective; dependent for its survival through cooperation and self denial of the greater good.

Feminist scholars and activists have to struggle to carve a separate identity for feminism in India by defining feminism as time and spatial to deny emergence and duplication of west. Indian women negotiate survival through an array of oppressive patriarchal structures of family (personal-age, ordinal status etc, relational-relationship to men through family of origin, marriage and procreation and patriarchal attributes-Dowry, siring sons etc.), kinship, caste, community, village, market and the state as compared to women in west, although several communities in India, such as the Nairs of Kerala, certain Maratha clans, and Bengali families exhibit matriarchal tendencies with the head of the family being the oldest women rather than the oldest man (also, Sikhs are relatively gender-neutral). Heterogeneity of Indian experience reveals there are multiple patriarchies so are feminisms. Hence feminism in India is not of singular theoretical orientations as compared to other concepts. It has changed over time in relation to historical and cultural realities, levels of consciousness, perceptions and actions of individual women and women as a group.

The widely used definition is, "An awareness of women's oppression and exploitation in society, at work and within the family, and conscious action by women and men to change this situation" Bhasin and Khan (1986). Acknowledging sexism in daily life and attempt to challenge and eliminate it through deconstructing mutually exclusive notions of femininity and masculinity as biologically determined categories opens way for equitable society for both men and women. The male and female dichotomy of polar opposites comprising of former oppressing later at all times is refuted in Indian context because it was men who initiated social reform movements against various social evils. Patriarchy is just one of the hierarchies. Relational hierarchies between women within the same family are more adverse. Here women are pitted against one another. Not all women are powerless at all times. Caste-community identities intensify all other hierarchies. The polytheistic Hindu pantheon provide revered images of women as unique and yet complementary to those of male deities.

FIRST PHASE OF FEMINISM IN INDIA (1850 - 1915)

Colonial venture into modernity brought concepts of democracy-equality and democratic-individual rights resulting in rise of concept of nationalism and introspection of discriminatory practices brought about social reform movements related to caste and gender relations. This phase can be identified as first wave of feminism in India. It was initiated by men to uproot the social evils of "Sati," widow immolation, widow remarriage, child marriage, age of consent, property rights and illiteracy through legal interventions. Women in this phase were categorized along with lower castes as subjects of social reforms and welfare instead of being recognized as autonomous agents of change. The emphasis was on recreating new space in pre existing feminine roles of caring. The women involved were those related to male activists, elite, western educated, upper caste Hindus.

SECOND PHASE OF FEMINISM (1915 - 1947)

During this period struggle against colonial rule intensified. Nationalism became pre-eminent cause. Tracing legitimacy of Indian superiority became tool of cultural revivalism resulting in essentializing model of Indian womanhood similar to that of Victorian, special yet separated from public space. Gandhi legitimized and expanded Indian women's public activities by initiating them in to non-violent civil disobedience movement against the Raj. He exalted their feminine roles of caring-self-abnegation, sacrifice and tolerance; and carved a niche for those in public space. Women-only organizations like All India Women's Conference (AIWC), National Federation of Indian Women (NFIW) emerged. Women were grappling with the issues of scope of women's political participation, women's franchise, communal award and leadership roles in political parties.

Women's participation in freedom struggle developed their critical consciousness about their role and rights in independent India. This resulted in induction of franchise and civic rights of women in Indian constitution. Provisions for women's upliftment through affirmative action, maternal health and child care provision-crèches, equal wage equal work etc. State acquired the patronizing role towards women. Women in India did not have to struggle for basic rights as did the women in west. The utopia ended soon when the social and cultural ideologies and structures failed to honor the newly acquired concepts of fundamental rights and democracy.

THIRD PHASE OF FEMINISM (AFTER 1974)

Role Models for Feminists in India

* Gargi
* Maitreyi
* Sultana Razia
* Imperial Queen mother Jijabai
* Rani Laxmibai
* Chandramukhi Basu
* Kadambini Ganguly
* Anandi Gopal Joshi
* Bhikaiji Cama
* Sucheta Kriplani
* Pritilata Waddedar
* Vijaya Lakshmi Pandit
* Rajkumari Amrit Kaur
* Sarojini Naidu
* Kiran Bedi

Gargi Vachaknavi

Gargi Vachaknavi was an ancient Indian female philosopher, born in the family of Garga. She was daughter of sage Vachaknavi. Gargi is mentioned in the Brihadaranyaka Upanishad. In Vedic literature, she is honored as one of the great natural philosophers. She was the daughter of sage Vachaknu. Gargi composed several hymns that questioned the origin of all existence. At brahmayajna, a philosophic congress organized by King Janak of Videha, she challenged the sage Yajnavalkya with perturbing questions on the atman (soul).

Maitreyi

Maitreyi was an ancient Indian female philosopher. She was one of the two wives of the sage Yajnavalkya, the other being Katyayani. Maitreyi was well-versed in the Hindu scriptures and was a brahmavadini. About ten hymns in Rig Veda are accredited to Maitreyi.

According to legend, Maitreyi really did not want to marry Yajnavalkya, but she wanted to live with him as a disciple and a spiritual companion to do sadhana. She went to Yajnavalkya's wife, Katyayani and expressed her desire to live with the sage. With Katyayani's consent, she became his companion.

Razia Sultana

Razia al-Din, "throne name" Jalâlat ud-Dîn Raziyâ, usually referred to in history as Razia Sultan or Razia Sultana, was born in 1205 and died in 1240. She was of Turkish Seljuks ancestry and like some other Muslim princesses of the time, she was trained to lead armies and administer kingdoms if necessary.

She succeeded her father Iltutmish to the Sultanate of Delhi in 1236. Iltutmish became the first sultan to appoint a woman as his successor when he designated his daughter Razia as his heir apparent. (According to one source, Iltumish's eldest son had initially been groomed as his successor, but had died prematurely.) But the Muslim nobility had no intention of acceding to Iltutmish's disregard of tradition in appointing a woman as heir, and after the sultan died on April 29, 1236, Razia's brother, Ruknuddin Feroze Shah, was elevated to the throne instead.

Ruknuddin's reign was short. With Iltutmish's widow Shah Turkaan for all practical purposes running the government, Ruknuddin abandoned himself to the pursuit of personal pleasure and debauchery, to the considerable outrage of the citizenry. On November 9, 1236, both Ruknuddin and his mother Shah Turkaan were put to death--after only six months in power.

With reluctance, the nobility next agreed to allow Razia to reign as sultana of Delhi. As a child and adolescent, Razia had had little contact with the women of the harem, so she had had little opportunity to learn the customary behavior of women in the Muslim society that she was born into. Even before she became queen--during her father's reign--she was reportedly preoccupied with the affairs of state. As sultana, Razia adopted men's dress; and contrary to custom, she would later show her face when she later rode an elephant into battle at the head of her army.

A shrewd politician, Razia managed to keep the nobles in check, while enlisting the support of the army and the populace. Her greatest accomplishment on the political front was to manipulate rebel factions into opposing each other. At that point, Razia seemed destined to become one of the most powerful rulers of the Delhi sultanate.

But the sultana miscounted the consequences that a special relationship with one of her Assyrian slaves, Jalal-ud-din Yaqut, would have for her reign. According to some accounts, Razia and Yaqut were lovers; other sources simply identify them as close confidants. In any case, before long she had aroused the jealousy of the Muslim nobility by the favoritism she displayed toward Yaqut. Eventually, the governor of Bhatinda, a childhood friend named Malik Ikhtiar-ud-din Altunia, rebelled, refusing any longer to accept Razia's authority.

A battle between Razia and Altunia ensued, with the result that Yaqut was killed and Razia taken prisoner. To escape death, Razia agreed to marry Altunia. Meanwhile, Razia's brother, Muiuddin Bahram Shah, had usurped the throne. After Altunia and Razia undertook to take back the sultanate from Bahram through battle, both Razia and her husband--neither one more than 30 years of age--were both killed on October 14, 1240 (some sources say October 13). Bahram, for his part, would later be dethroned for incompetence.

Razia's Legacy

As sultana, Razia reportedly sought to abolish the tax on non-Muslims but met opposition from the nobility. By way of response, Razia is said to have pointed out that the spirit of religion was more important than its parts, and that even the Muslim Prophet spoke against overburdening the non-Muslims.

On another occasion, Razia reportedly tried to appoint an Indian Muslim convert from Hinduism to an official position but again ran into opposition from the nobles. In this case she yielded, having concluded that the bonds of Islam were weaker than old prejudices.

Razia was reportedly devoted to the cause of her empire and to her subjects. There is no record that she made any attempt to remain aloof from her subjects, rather it appears she preferred to mingle among them. Her tolerance of Hinduism would later bring her criticism from Muslim historians.

Razia established schools, academies, centers for research, and public libraries that included the works of ancient philosophers along with the Koran and the Traditions of the Prophet. Hindu works in the sciences, philosophy, astronomy, and literature were reportedly studied in schools and colleges.

Razia's Tomb

Today Razia's unpretentious tomb lies among the narrow lanes of Old Delhi in Northern India. Crumbling and covered by dust and grime, the tomb has clearly suffered the ravages of time. The grave is surrounded on all sides by unattractive residential buildings. Meanwhile modern-day encroachers have placed plastic sheets around the tomb and started to live in it, turning it into an urban ghetto.

In the thirteenth century, the site of the tomb was a jungle, and no one knows how Razia's body ended up where it lies today. Though a second grave accompanies Razia's, the identity of the occupant is unknown. Some of the local residents have turned the tomb into a place of worship, where prayers are conducted five times each day.

-Razia refused to be addressed to as Sultana because it meant "wife of a sultan". She would only answer to the title "Sultan".

Jijabai

Jijabai was the mother of Shivaji, founder of the Maratha Empire. She was a daughter of Lakhuji Jadhav, a prominent grandee of Sindkhed in the present-day Buldhana district of Maharashtra State. As per the customs of that age, she was wed at an early age to Shahaji Bhosale, a nobleman and military commander under the Adil Shahi sultans of Bijapur in present-day Karnataka. She was his second wife.

Jijabai was the mother of eight children, six daughters and two sons. Shivaji was the younger of her sons. Jijabai was well known for her chivalry and character.

On Mission

She wholeheartly supported her husband's cause. Shahaji had tried to establish maratha state on the ruin of the erstwhile Nizamshahi sultanate. However he was defeated by the combined forces of Mughals and Adilshahi. As per the treaty he was forced to move south. In order to continue the struggle, he deputed her as queen regent. She was chosen for this because of her ability as a warrior and administrator. This has been the tradition of Maratha women since time immemorial. At that time Shivaji was 14 years old and so accompanied his mother.

The elder son Sambhaji remained with their father. Shivaji left Banglore along with her mother, a council of ministers and chosen military commanders. Against this background, Shivaji took oath at the temple of lord Raireshwar. The rest of the story is well known. Her elder son Sambhaji was killed in a battle with Afzul Khan of the Adil Shahi court. Shivaji killed Afzul Khan and took revenge.

When Shahaji died Jijabai tried to committ suttee but Shivaji stopped her from doing so by request.

Jijabai is widely credited with raising Shivaji in a manner that led to his future greatness. She gave a human touch to Shivaji's personality. His policy towards captured women reflects her influence. She died immediately after the coronation of Shivaji, fulfilling her mission.

It is worth mentioning that apart from her, Rukmini (wife of Krishna), Damayanti (wife of Nala), Lopamudra (wife of sage agasti) were princesses from Bhoj Yadavas of Vidarbha. All four princesses are well known for their versite personality and character.

Rani Lakshmibai

Lakshmibai, The Rani of Jhansi (c. 1828 – 17 June 1858), the queen of the Maratha-ruled princely state of Jhansi in North India, was one of the leading figures of the Indian rebellion of 1857, and a symbol of resistance to British rule in India.

She was born at Kashi and died at Gwalior. Her childhood name was Manikarnika. She is sometimes referred to as the Boudicca of India.

Lakshmi Bai was a Maharashtrian born sometime around 1828 at Kashi (presently known as Varanasi). An alternate date of 19 November 1835 was asserted by D. B. Parasnis in his biography of the Rani. However, no other credible historian agrees with this date and all the evidence points to 1828. The simplest and most direct evidence comes via John Lang. In his account of his meeting with the Rani in 1854 he mentions that her vakil said she was a woman of about 26 years.

Her father Moropanth Tambey was a Karhade Brahmin and her mother Bhagirathibai was cultured, intelligent and religious. Born Manikarnika, she was affectionately called Manu in her family. Manu lost her mother at the age of four, and responsibility of looking after the young girl fell to her father. She completed her education and martial training, which included horse riding, fencing and shooting, when she was still a child.

She was married to Raja Gangadhar Rao Newalkar, the Maharaja of Jhansi in 1842, and became the queen of Jhansi. After their marriage, she was given the name Lakshmi Bai. The ceremony of the marriage was performed at the Ganesh Mandir, the temple of Lord Ganesha situated in the old city of Jhansi. Rani Lakshmi Bai gave birth to a son in 1851, but this child died when he was about four months old.

In 1853 Gangadhar Rao fell very ill and he was persuaded to adopt a child. To ensure that the British would not be able to contest the adoption, the Rani had it witnessed by the local British representatives. Maharaja Gangadhar Rao expired the following day, 21 November 1853.

Annexation

At that time, Lord Dalhousie was the Governor General of British India. Though little Damodar Rao, adopted son of late Maharaja Gangadhar Rao and Rani Lakshmi Bai, was Maharaja's heir and successor under Hindu tradition, the British rulers rejected Rani's claim that Damodar Rao was their legal heir. Lord Dalhousie decided to annex the state of Jhansi under the Doctrine of Lapse.

The Rani then did the unprecedented: she sought the advice of a British lawyer, John Lang, and appealed her case in London. Although these petitions were well-argued, they were ultimately rejected. The British Indian authorities clearly sought to punish Rani for her presumptuous behavior.[citation needed] They confiscated the state jewels and deducted her husband's debts from her annual pension of Rs. 60,000. She was required to leave Jhansi fort for the Rani Mahal in Jhansi town, as well. But Rani Lakshmi Bai was determined to defend Jhansi. She proclaimed her decision with the famous words: Mi mahji Jhansi nahi dehnar (I will not give up my Jhansi).

The war

Jhansi became a center of the rebellion upon the outbreak of violence in 1857. Rani Lakshmi Bai started strengthening the defense of Jhansi and assembled a volunteer army. Women were recruited as well as men and given military training. Rani was accompanied by her generals. Many from the local population volunteered for service in the army ranks, with the popular support for her cause on the rise.

In September and October of 1857, the Rani led the successful defense of Jhansi from the invading armies of the neighboring rajas of Datia and Orchha.

In January of 1858, the British Army started its advance on Jhansi, and in March laid siege to the city. After two weeks of fighting the British captured the city, but the Rani escaped in the guise of a man, strapping her adopted son Damodar Rao closely on her back. She fled to Kalpi where she joined Tatya Tope.

During the battle for Gwalior the Rani met her death on 17 June. During this battle the Rani's original horse was mortally wounded. He had to be replaced by a younger, more energetic, but less trained horse.

The folklore surrounding her during the war is that during the battle the Rani was trying to escape and two British officers followed her. The horse reached a cliff and being insufficiently trained, could not pass over it. The British set upon her by surrounding her. As she was cornered, she knew there was only one option to take was to jump off which she did. A Brahmin, who found her, carefully took her into his ashram. She lay there unconscious for a moment then her last words were "Jai Hind!", meaning victory to India. In actual fact, most sources have the Rani being shot or run through with a saber and there is no mention of a cliff. It is also unlikely that the many princes who led the Mutiny were in any way more than peripherally concerned with the concept of a united India.

All were uniformly concerned with the loss of their personal powers and privileges, and at most, with regional issues. Indeed Laksmi Bai's main objective throughout the Mutiny seems to have been to secure the throne of Jhansi for her adopted son. For a considerable length of time after the start of the Mutiny, she was in correspondence with the British and professed to be on the British side, stating in her letters that she hoped in return that the East India Company would eventually restore all privileges to her son. There are also allegations that Lakshmi Bai did not do enough to prevent the massacre of the British garrison at Jhansi. It is probable that soldiers in her pay took part in the massacre.

The British captured Gwalior three days later. In his report of the battle for Gwalior, General Rose commented that the Rani had been "the bravest and the best" of the rebels. Because of her unprecedented bravery, courage and wisdom and her progressive views on women's empowerment in 19th century India, and due to her sacrifices, she became an icon of Indian nationalist movement.

Epilogue

The fall of Jhansi and the death of Rani Lakshmibai was the last series of the resistance to British Raj under the Sepoy Mutiny. Its immediate effects included:

* Due to her bravery, she became a national hero and the epitome of female bravery in India. When the Indian National Army, formed by Subhash C. Bose of Indian prisoners of war to fight the British created its first female unit, it was named after her.
* Her father, Moropant Tambe, was captured and hanged a few days after the fall of Jhansi.
* Her adopted son, Damodar Rao, was given a pension by the British Raj, although he never received his inheritance.
* The administration of an undivided India passed on from the East India Company to the British crown.
* The Rani was memorialized in bronze statues at both Jhansi and Gwalior, both of which portray her in equestrian style.

Chandramukhi Basu

Chandramukhi Basu, who was a Bengali speaking Christian from Dehradun, which was located in the (then known as) United Provinces of Agra and Oudh, was one of the first two female graduates of the British Empire. Along with Kadambini Ganguly, she received her Bachelor's degree in Arts from the Bethune College, an affiliate college of the University of Calcutta, India in 1883.

Early Life

The daughter of Bhuban Mohan Bose, she passed the First Arts examination from Dehradun Native Christian School in

1880. Till then Bethune School did not admit non-Hindu girls. The rule was relaxed and she was admitted for the degree course, along with Kadambini Ganguly. After her graduation, she was the only and first woman to pass MA from Calcutta Univerity in 1884.

Career

She started her career as a lecturer in Bethune College (it was still part of Bethune School) in 1886. The college was separated from the school in 1888. She became the principal, thus becoming the first female head of an undergraduate academic establishment in South Asia.

She retired in 1891 because of bad health and spent the rest of her life in Dehradun.

Sisters

Two of her sisters, Bidhumukhi and Bindubasini, were also renowned. Bidhumukhi Bose and Virginia Mary Mitra (Nandi) were the first two woman medical graduates from Calcutta Medical College. They passed out in 1890. Thereafter, Bindubasini Bose passed out from Calcutta Medical College in 1891.

Kadambini Ganguly

Kadambini Ganguly (1861 – 3 October 1923) was one of the first female graduates of the British Empire and the first female physician of South Asia to be trained in European medicine.

Early Life

The daughter of Brahmo reformer Braja Kishore Basu, she was born at Bhagalpur, Bihar in British India. The family was from Chandsi, in Barisal which is now in Bangladesh. Her father was headmaster of Bhagalpur School. He and Abhay Charan Mallick started the movement for women's emancipation at Bhagalpur, establishing the women's organisation Bhagalpur Mahila Samiti in 1863, the first in India.

Kadambini started her education at Banga Mahila Vidyalaya and while at Bethune School (established by Bethune) in 1878 became the first woman to pass the University of Calcutta entrance examination. It was partly in recognition of her efforts that Bethune College first introduced FA (First Arts), and then graduation courses in 1883. She and Chandramukhi Basu became the first graduates from Bethune College, and in the process became the first female graduates in the country and in the entire British Empire.

Medical Education and Profession

Ganguly studied medicine at the Calcutta Medical College. In 1886, she was awarded a GBMC (Graduate of Bengal Medical College) degree, which gave her the right to practise. She thus became the first Indian woman doctor qualified to practice western medicine. Abala Bose passed entrance in 1881 but was refused admission to the medical college and went to Madras (now Chennai) to study medicine but never graduated.

Kadambini overcame some opposition from the teaching staff, and orthodox sections of society. She went to the United Kingdom in 1892 and returned to India after qualifying as LRCP (Edinburgh), LRCS (Glasgow), and GFPS (Dublin). After working for a short period in Lady Dufferin Hospital, she started her own private practice.

Social Activities

In 1883 she married the Brahmo reformer and leader of women's emancipation Dwarka Nath Ganguly. They were actively involved in female emancipation and social movements to improve work conditions of female coal miners in eastern India. She was one of the six female delegates to the fifth session of the Indian National Congress in 1889, and even organized the Women's Conference in Calcutta in 1906 in the aftermath of the partition of Bengal. In 1908, she had also organized and presided over a Calcutta meeting for expressing sympathy with Satyagraha-inspired Indian laborers in Transvaal, South Africa. She formed an association to collect money with the help of fundraisers to assist the workers. In

1914 she presided over the meeting of the Sadharan Brahmo Samaj, which was held in Calcutta to honour Mahatma Gandhi during his Calcutta visit.

As the mother of eight children she had to devote considerable time to her household affairs. She was deft in needlework.

The noted American historian David Kopf [2] has written, "Ganguli's wife, Kadambini, was appropriately enough the most accomplished and liberated Brahmo woman of her time. From all accounts, their relationship was most unusual in being founded on mutual love, sensitivity and intelligence... Mrs. Ganguli's case was hardly typical even among the more emancipated Brahmo and Christian women in contemporary Bengali society. Her ability to rise above circumstances and to realize her potential as a human being made her a prize attraction to Sadharan Brahmos dedicated ideologically to the liberation of Bengal's women."

Anandi Gopal Joshi

Anandi Gopal Joshi (or Anandibai) (March 31, 1865-February 26, 1887) was the first Indian woman to obtain a medical degree in the Western hemisphere. She was one of the first Indian women to be trained in Western system of medicine. Many sources claim that she was the first India's first woman doctor. A fictionalized account of her life has been depicted in the novel "Anandi Gopal", written by SJ Joshi.

Early Life

Joshi was born as Yamuna Joshi (Yamunabai) at Thane near Mumbai, in an orthodox wealthy Brahmin family. She suffered from pockmarks. Aged 9, she was married to a postal clerk, Gopalrao Joshi. Gopalrao, also a Brahmin, was a widower and almost twenty years her senior. After the marriage, Yamuna was renamed as Anandi, according to Maharashtrian traditions.

Gopalrao worked as a postal clerk in Kalyan. Later, he was transferred to Alibag, and finally to Calcutta (now Kolkata). He was a progressive thinker, and supported the education of women-then not very prevalent in India. It was common for Brahmins to learn Sanskrit, but Lokhitawadi's Shat Patre had convinced Gopalrao that Sanskrit was no longer of much use. He considered English to be more important. He noticed his wife's interest in learning and helped her to learn English.

At the age of 14, Joshi gave birth to a boy. The child survived only for ten days, owing to the paucity of medical care available. This incident was a turning point in Joshi's life and inspired her to become a doctor.

Towards a Medical Career

Gopalrao encouraged his wife to study medicine. In 1880, he sent a letter to Royal Wilder, a well-known American missionary, expressing Anandi's interest in studying medicine in the United States, and inquiring about a suitable post there for himself. Wilder offered to help if the couple converted to Christianity. This was not acceptable to the Joshis.

Wilder published the correspondence in his publication, Princeton's Missionary Review. It was read by Theodicia E. Carpenter, a resident of Roselle, New Jersey, while waiting to see her dentist. She was impressed by Joshi's desire to learn medicine, and by Gopalrao's support for his wife. She wrote to them, offering accommodation to Joshi in America. This began a series of letters between Joshi and Carpenter, in which they discussed Hindu culture and religion, among other things.

While Gopalrao and Joshi were in Calcutta, Joshi's general health was declining. She suffered from weakness, constant headaches, occasional fever, and sometimes breathlessness. Carpenter sent her medicines from America, without results. In 1883, Gopalrao was transferred to Serampore. It was here that he decided to send Joshi to America alone. Joshi was apprehensive, but Gopalrao convinced her by saying that she should set an example for other women.

A Dr Thorborn and his wife, who was also a doctor, suggested Joshi apply to the Woman's Medical College of Pennsylvania. When Joshi's decision became known, she was rejected by Hindu society. She was spat at in public and had stones thrown at her. Many Christians supported her decision, but they wanted her to convert to Christianity.

Eventually, Joshi addressed the community at Serampore College Hall, explaining her decision to go to America and obtain a medical degree. She discussed the persecution she and her husband had endured. She stressed the need for Hindu female doctors in India, and talked about her goal of opening a medical college for women in India. She also pledged that she would not convert from Hinduism. After her speech was published, financial contributions started coming in from all over India. The Viceroy of India contributed 200 rupees towards funds for her education. However, the money was not enough, and Joshi had to sell her gold bangles to fund her travel and education.

In America

Joshi travelled to New York from Calcutta by ship, chaperoned by two English female acquaintances of Dr Thorborn. In New York, Carpenter received her in June 1883. Joshi wrote to the Women's Medical College of Pennsylvania, asking to be admitted to their medical program, which was the first women's medical program in the world. Rachel L. Bodley, the dean of the college, enrolled her.

Joshi began her medical education at the age of 19. In America, her already declining health was worsened by the cold weather and unfamiliar diet. She contracted tuberculosis. Her friends sent her to Colorado Springs for her health, but it failed to improve her condition.

She submitted a thesis on "Obstetrics among the Aryan Hindoos". When she graduated with an M.D. on March 11, 1886, Queen Victoria sent a congratulatory message.

Return to India

Joshi's husband and her friends advised her to settle in the United States, but she insisted on returning to India. Before she returned to India, the princely state of Kolhapur, appointed her the Physician-in-charge of the female ward of the Albert

Edward Hospital. On October 9, 1886, she sailed from New York. She returned to India, and was met with a hero's welcome. The newspapers closely monitored her health.

Joshi died in Poona at any early age of 22, in her mother's arms. Her death was mourned throughout India. Her ashes were sent to Carpenter, who placed them in her family cemetery in Poughkeepsie, New York.

A fictionalized account of her experiences was depicted in the Marathi novel Anandi Gopal, written by Shrikrishna Janardan Joshi.

Bhikaiji Cama

Bhikaiji Rustom Cama (Madam Cama, Madame Cama) (September 24, 1861-August 13, 1936) was a prominent figure in the Indian Nationalist Movement.

Bhikaiji Rustom Cama was born Bhikai Sorab Patel on 24th September, 1861 in Bombay (now Mumbai) into a large, well-off Parsi family. Her parents, Sorabji and Jaijibai Patel, were well-known in the city, where her father Sorabji Framji Patel-a lawyer by training and a merchant by profession-was an influential member of the Parsi community. The father doted on his little girl, and affectionately called her "Munni".

Like many Parsi girls of the time, Bhikaiji attended Alexandra Native Girl's English Institution. Bhikaiji was by all accounts a diligent, disciplined child, with a flair for languages and an interest in the personalities of the nationalist movement(s).

On August 3, 1885, she married Rustom Cama, a wealthy, pro-British lawyer with a desire to enter politics. It was not a happy marriage, and Bhikaiji spent most of her time and energy in philanthropic activities and social work.

In October 1896, the Bombay Presidency was first hit by famine, and shortly thereafter by bubonic plague. Bhikaiji joined one of the many teams working out of Grant Medical College (which would subsequently become Haffkine's plague vaccine research center), in an effort to provide care for the afflicted, and (later) to inoculate the healthy. She contracted the plague herself, but survived. Severely weakened, she set sail for Europe for subsequent medical care and recuperation in 1902. In London, she received word that her return to India would be prevented unless she sign a statement promising not to participate in nationalist activities. She refused, and remained in exile in Europe until shortly before her death (at Parsi General Hospital in Bombay) in 1936.

While in London, she served as private secretary to Dadabhai Naoroji, the first Asian to be elected to the British House of Commons, and the first to publicly demand independence from Great Britain.

In Paris she came in contact with other notable members of the movement for Indian sovereignty, and would come to clandestinely (in Holland) publish and distribute revolutionary literature for the movement. While in France, the British Government requested her extradition, but the French Government refused to cooperate. In return, the British Government seized Cama's inheritance. Lenin reportedly invited her to reside in Russia, but she did not accept.

Influenced by Christabel Pankhurst and the Suffragette movement, Bhikaiji Cama was vehement in her support for gender equality. Speaking in Cairo, Egypt in 1910, she asked, "I see here the representatives of only half the population of Egypt. May I ask where is the other half? Sons of Egypt, where are the daughters of Egypt? Where are your mothers and sisters? Your wives and daughters?"

Bhikaiji Cama is best known for having unfurled a "Flag of Indian Independence" on August 22, 1907, at the International Socialist Conference in Stuttgart, Germany. That flag, a slight modification of the Calcutta Flag, was co-designed by Cama, Veer Savarkar and Shyamji Krishna Varma, and would later serve as a template upon which the current national flag of India is based.

At the conference, she described the devastating effects of a famine that had struck the subcontinent, and made an appeal for human rights, equality and for Indian independence: "This flag is of India's independence. Behold, it is born. It is already sanctified by the blood of martyred Indian youth. I call upon you, gentlemen, to rise and salute the flag of Indian independence. In the name of this flag I appeal to lovers of freedom all over the world to cooperate with this flag in freeing one-fifth of the human race".

One nationalist legend involving Bhikaiji Cama goes like this:

Veer Savarkar was in custody (aboard the "Morena") for his nationalist stance. As the story goes, Savarkar evaded his captors and jumped overboard in an attempt to escape. Cama saw him go overboard, but misunderstood it to be an accident. She jumped in after him (to save him as she thought), and attracted enough attention to result in Savarkar's recapture.

Another variation of the story (possibly true), goes like this:

Veer Savarkar had been arrested in London for nationalist activities and was on his way back to India for trial. Aboard the "Morena" in Marseilles Harbour, he wiggled out of a porthole window and jumped into the sea. Reaching shore, he expected to find Cama and others waiting for him (who got there late), but ran into the local constabulary instead. Unable to communicate his predicament to the French authorities without Cama's help, he was returned to British custody.

Several Indian cities have streets and places named after Bhikaiji Cama. On January 26th 1962, the Indian Posts and Telegraphs Department issued a stamp in her honor. The Indian Coast Guard has a ship named after her.

Sucheta Kriplani

Sucheta Kriplani (born Sucheta Mazumdar) (1908-1974) was an Indian freedom fighter and politician. She became the first woman to be elected Chief Minister of a state.

Early Life

She was born in Ambala, Haryana to a Bengali family. Her father, S.N. Majumdar though a government doctor was a nationalist. Educated at Indraprastha College and St.Stephen's College, Delhi she became a lecturer at the Banaras Hindu University. In 1936, she married socialist,Acharya Kriplani and became involved with the Indian National Congress.

Freedom Movement and Independence

Like her contemporaries Aruna Asaf Ali and Usha Mehta, she came to the forefront during the Quit India Movement. She later worked closely with Mahatma Gandhi during the Partition riots. She accompanied him to Noakhali in 1946. She was one of the few women who were elected to the Constituent Assembly and was part of the subcommittee that drafted the Indian Constitution.

On 15th August, 1947 she sang Vande Mataram in the Independence Session of the Constituent Assembly.

Post Independence

After independence she remained involved with politics in U.P. She was elected to the Lok Sabha in 1952 and 1957 and served as a Minister of State for Small Scale Industries. In 1962, she was elected to the U.P Assembly from Kanpur and served in the Cabinet in 1962. In 1963, she became the Chief Minister of Uttar Pradesh, the first woman to hold that position in any Indian state. The highlight of her tenure was the firm handling of a state employees strike. The first-ever strike by the state employees which continued for 62 days took place during her regime. She relented only when the employees' leaders agreed for compromise. Although the wife of a socialist, Kriplani cemented her reputation as a firm administrator by refusing their demand for pay hike.

She retired from politics in 1971 and remained in seclusion till her death in 1974.

Pritilata Waddedar

Pritilata Waddedar was an anti-British pro-India revolutionary in East Bengal, (then part of Province of Bengal in pre-independence India), now in Bangladesh.

Born in Chittagong in 1911, she was a meritorious student at the Dr. Khastagir Government Girls' School of Chittagong and passed the matriculation examination in the first division in 1927. She continued her education in Eden College, Dhaka and in 1929, she passed the Intermediate examinations securing the first place among all the candidates from Dhaka Board. Two years later, Pritilata graduated in Philosophy with distinction from Bethune College of Kolkata.

In early 1930s, Pritilata joined Mastarda Surya Sen's armed resistance movement. In 1932, Surya Sen planned an attack on the Pahartali European Club, which bore the notorious sign 'Dogs and Indians not allowed'. He assigned Pritilata to lead a team that would attack the Club on September 23, 1932. Members of the team were instructed to carry potassium cyanide with them so that in case they were caught by police they could swallow it before the arrest. The raid was successful but Pritilata, dressed as a man was trapped without a way of escape on that fateful night. She committed suicide by swallowing the cyanide, thus ending her short endeavor in fighting for freedom of her country.

Vijaya Lakshmi Pandit

Vijaya Lakshmi Nehru Pandit (1900-1990) was an Indian diplomat and politician, sister of Indian Prime Minister Jawaharlal Nehru, and the first female President of the United Nations General Assembly.

In 1921 she married Ranjit Sitaram Pandit. She was the first Indian woman to hold a cabinet post. In 1937 she was elected to the provincial legislature of the United Provinces and designated minister of local self-government and public health. She held the latter post until 1939 and again from 1946 to 1947. In 1946, she was elected to the Constituent Assembly from the United Provinces.

Following India's independence from the British in 1947, she entered the diplomatic service and became India's ambassador to several different countries: the Soviet Union from 1947 to 1949, the United States and Mexico from 1949 to 1951, Ireland from 1955 to 1961 (during which time she was also the Indian High Commissioner to the United Kingdom), and Spain from 1958 to 1961. Between 1946 and 1968 she also headed the Indian delegation to the United Nations.

In India, she served as governor of Maharashtra from 1962 until 1964, after which she was elected to the Indian Lok Sabha from Phulpur, her brother's former constituency. She held office from 1964 to 1968. Pandit was a harsh critic of her niece, Indira Gandhi, after Gandhi became Prime Minister in 1966, and she retired from active politics after relations soured between them. Upon retiring, she moved to Dehradun in the Doon Valley in the Himalayan foothills.

In 1979 she was appointed the Indian representative to the UN Human Rights Commission, after which she retired from public life. Her writings include The Evolution of India (1958) and The Scope of Happiness: A Personal Memoir (1979).

Her daughter Nayantara Sahgal, who later settled in her mother's house in Dehradun, is a well-known novelist.

Rajkumari Amrit Kaur

Rajkumari Amrit Kaur (2nd February 1889, Lucknow – 2nd October 1964) was the first female Indian Cabinet Minister. She was born into the princely family of Kapurthala of undivided India and became an eminent Gandhian, social activist and freedom fighter. Lakshmi N. Menon had described her, as "the master craft of Gandhi is conspicuously visible in the case of Amrit Kaur who gave up her princely ways and habits in favour of service for the nation." For many years she remained close to the select group of leaders fighting for the freedom of India, and after India's independence she became the health minister of India. She also remained active in many social activities.

Early Life

Rajkumari Amrit Kaur was born on 2nd February 1889 in Lucknow (Uttar Pradesh, India), and belonged to a princely family. She was the only daughter of her parents, Raja Harnam Singh and Rani Harnam Singh. Her mother was a Bengali

Presbyterian Christian. She had seven brothers, and the environment in her home was generally strict and disciplined one. Rajkumari inherited Christianity as her religion, and her early education was in England in a school at Sherborne, Dorsetshire, and later studies at the Oxford. She was also a good player of tennis and won several prizes. With her family and educational background, she could have led a life of affluence and luxury. However, when she returned to India, She got attracted towards the freedom movement and became a social worker.

Her father Raja Sir Harnam Singh was reputed as a "pious and pure" Christian. Harman Singh was the last ruling prince of Kapurthala in the Punjab region, and enjoyed the goodwill and confidence of many leaders of the Indian National Congress party, including Gopal Krishna Gokhale, one of the most prominent leaders of his time. Many other political leaders also visited the Raja, and Amrit Kaur became interested in the freedom struggle and learnt about the activities of the freedom fighters and about Mahatma Gandhi. She saw Mahatma Gandhi for the first time in Bombay (now called Mumbai), and was immensely influenced by his words.

The Jallianwala Bagh Massacre of 1919 resulted into killing of unarmed civilians by the troops of the British Raj, and this incidence convinced her about necessity for India to become a free nation. Although her parents were against her joining Mahatma Gandhi at his ashram due to a life of austerities there, she remained convinced to be part of the struggle for the freedom of India. She started spinning khadi, and participated in social work in Jallandhar and later among the Harijans of Simla.

Inspired by Mahatma Gandhi, she joined the Indian National Congress party, and became socially and politically active. She participated in a number of movements initiated by Mahatma Gandhi for the freedom of India, including a 240 mile march led by Gandhi in March 1930, known as the Dandi march. During the march, Rajkumari was arrested and imprisoned by the authorities of the British Raj.

As a Gandhian

After her father's death, she left her home and came to live in Mahatma Gandhi's ashram in 1934. She started wearing clothes made of khadi, and became an active disciple of Mahatma Gandhi. Sometime, visitors from Europe and the USA would be amazed to learn an Indian princesses living in the ashram in an environment of austerities.

She was assigned the role of Mahatma Gandhi's English language secretary, and it was a challenging assignment. Mahatma Gandhi received and enormous quantity of mails, and he himself used to write more than 160 notes in own hands, and his other secretaries (namely, Mahadev Desai and Pyarelal) handled thousands of mails every week. Beside these, the secretaries were also required to manage innumerable editorials, essays, and public statements. Generally Mahatma Gandhi was tender to her in the early days, but was a strict disciplinarian.

She once recalled that she delivered a note written by Mahatma Gandhi to a wrong person, and this made the Mahatma very unhappy. However, at the same time Mahatma Gandhi used to care for all the people around her, and on her birthday she received a hand written note from Mahatma Gandhi which read: "an ideal secretary keeps her chief straight when he is going astray. She hovers over him, watches all movements about him... picks up his papers, even those torn... lest he might have torn something important, by mistake. She leaves after him and seeks what he left behind... and if not owned by anyone else, collects it. Follow the spirit of this note and you will be the ideal secretary. This is my birthday present, which goes loaded with all the good wishes that I am capable of conveying... Love, Bapu." She continued to serve Mahatma Gandhi as one of his secretaries for sixteen years.

As a representative of the Indian National Congress, she was sent on a mission of goodwill to Bannu, Northwest Frontier Province. The British government of the Raj arrested her, charging her with sedition, and she was convicted and imprisoned on 16th July 1937. In 1942, she again became active in the Quit India Movement; led many protest rallies, and in one of such rallies in Kalka (Punjab) suffered injuries when the troops charged the protesters. She was arrested and imprisoned again.

She was a co-founder of the All India Women's Conference in 1927, and became its secretary in 1930. During 1931-33 she served as the president of the Women's Association. She also championed the cause of universal suffrage, and espoused and testified before the Lothian Committee on Indian franchise and constitutional reforms, and before the Joint Select Committee of Parliament on Indian constitutional reforms.

In 1938 she was elected as the president of All India Women's Conference. She had also served as the Chairperson of the All India Women's Education Fund Association and as a member of the Executive Committee of Lady Irwin College, New Delhi. She was an appointed as a member (the first women to be so appointed) by the British Raj to the Advisory Board of Education, a position which she resigned in the wake of the Quit India Movement. She was sent as a member of the Indian delegation to participate in UNESCO's conferences in London (1945), and in Paris (1946). She also served as a member of the Board of Trustees of the All India Spinners' Association.

She was committed to Mahatma Gandhi's objective of making India a free nation, and at the same time continued to be active in elimination of several bad practices of the Indian society, and such practices included early or child marriage, system of purdah both among the Muslim and Hindu women, illiteracy. She articulated her views on these issues in these words: "the abolition of earl marriage and purdah, therefore, will not only improve the health of millions of women but will remove two of the main obstacles in the way of the spread of female education. Needless to say that the position of the widows in Hindu homes, marriage laws and the laws relating to the inheritance of property by women need radical alteration."

She also actively espoused the cause of female education, and believed in reforms in the education of Indian women. In one of the women's conferences, she had presented her views as follows: "in the realm of educational reform, we have urged ever since our inception that there should be free and compulsory education. Again, as far as proper facilities for the female education are concerned until such time as universal, free and compulsory primary education as well as an adequate supply of infant and girl's schools equipped with trained women teachers are introduced, we must continue to do our utmost to have the system of education in our exiting institutions changed."

Post-independence

After India's independence, Amrit Kaur became part of Jawaharlal Nehru's first Cabinet; she was the first woman to hold Cabinet rank. She was assigned the Ministry of Health, and was the only Indian Christian in the Cabinet. She was also elected the president of World Health Assembly in 1950, a position held by only two women in the first 25 years of the WHO's history.

She was also the moving force behind the conceptualization and building of the All India Institute of Medical Sciences in New Delhi, and for establishing this institute she secured aid from New Zealand, funds form the West Germany for books, equipments form the Sweden, and assistance for a rehabilitation centre from the Vocational Rehabilitation Centre of US to establish a rehabilitation centre. She also secured aid from the Rockefeller Foundation and Punjab Government for the medical Community Block.

She and her brother even donated their ancestral property and house named Manorville (Simla, Himachal Pradesh, India) to serve as a holiday home for the staff and nurses of the institute. She functioned as the Chairperson of the Indian Red Cross society for fourteen years, and during her leadership, the Indian Red Cross did a number of pioneering works in the tribal belts and hinterland of India.

She continued to be the Health Minister of India until 1957, after which she retired from ministerial activity but remained a member of the Rajya Sabha until her death on 2nd October, 1964. However, until her death, she continued to hold charge of the Presidentship of the All India Institute of Medical Sciences, and the Tuberculosis Association and the Chairperson of the Indian Red Cross and St. John's Ambulance Corps. Rajkumari Amrit Kaur remained a spinster all her life.

Quotes

About Harijans: "It is a crying shame that the people who cater for our services are relegated in most towns to live in the most abominable dwellings—if, indeed we can call their hovels by this name."

About Child Marriage: "Child marriage is eating as a canker into the vitality of our national life. Girls become mothers while they are children themselves, and bring into the world off—springs, who are, in the very nature of things, the victims of disease and ill health."

Sarojini Naidu

Sarojini Naidu (February 13, 1879-March 2, 1949), known as Bharatiya Kokila (The Nightingale of India), was a child prodigy, freedom fighter, and poet. Naidu was the first Indian woman to become the President of the Indian National Congress and the first woman to become the governor of a state in India.

Early Life and Family

Sarojini Chattopadhyaya was born in Hyderabad, India as the eldest daughter of scientist-philosopher, Aghornath Chattopadhyaya, and Varada Sundari Devi, a poetess. Her father was the founder of the Nizam College. She learnt to speak Urdu, Telugu, English, Persian and Bengali. Her favorite poet was P.B. Shelley.

She attained national fame for entering Madras University at the age of twelve. At sixteen, she travelled to England to study first at King's College London, and Girton College, Cambridge.

At the age of 17, she met Dr. Muthyala Govindarajulu Naidu and fell in love with him. He was from South India. After finishing her studies at the age of 19, she married him during the time when inter-caste marriages were not allowed. Her marriage was a very happy one. They were married by the Brahmo Marriage Act (1872), in Madras in 1898. They had 4 children: Jayasurya, Padmaja, Randheer, and Leelamani.

In the Freedom Struggle

She joined the Indian independence movement, in the wake of the aftermath of partition of Bengal in 1905. During 1903-17 Sarojini came into contact with Gopal Krishna Gokhale, Rabindranath Tagore, Muhammad Ali Jinnah, Annie Besant, C. P. Ramaswami Iyer, Mohandas Gandhi and Jawaharlal Nehru.

From 1915 to 1918 she lectured all over India on welfare of youth, dignity of labour, women's emancipation and nationalism. After meeting Jawaharlal Nehru in 1916, she took up the cause of the indigo workers of Champaran. In 1925 she was elected as the President of the Congress, the first Indian woman to hold the post.

In March 1919, the Britain | British government passed the Rowlatt Act by which the possession of seditious documents was deemed illegal. Mohandas Gandhi organized the Non-Cooperation Movement to protest and Naidu was the first to join the movement which the government worked to suppress.

In July 1919, Naidu became the Home Rule League's ambassador to England. In July 1920 she returned to India and on August 1, Mahatma Gandhi declared the Non-Cooperation Movement. In January 1924, she was one of the two Indian National Congress delegates at the East African Indian Congress.

Naidu arrived in New York in October 1928 and was concerned with the unjust treatment of the African Americans and the Amerindians. Upon her return to India she became a member of Congress Working Committee.

On January 26, 1930 the National Congress proclaimed its independence from the British Empire. On May 5, Mohandas Gandhi was arrested. Naidu was arrested shortly thereafter and was in jail for several months. She, along with Gandhi, was released on January 31, 1931. Later that year, they were again arrested.

Naidu was eventually released due to her poor health and Gandhi was released in 1933. In 1931, she participated in the Round Table Summit, along with Gandhiji and Pundit Malaviyaji. In 1942, she was arrested during the "Quit India" protest and stayed in jail for 21 months with Gandhiji. Naidu shared a warm relationship with Mohandas Gandhi, even calling him "Mickey Mouse".

At the Asian Relations Conference of March 1947, Naidu presided over the Steering Committee.

On August 15, 1947, with the independence of India, Naidu became the Governor of Uttar Pradesh, India's first woman governor and she died in office in 1949.

Poetry, Writings and Quotes

In 1905, the first volume of her collection of poems was published as The Golden Threshold. Two more volumes were published: The Bird of Time (1912) and The Broken Wing in (1917).

Sarojini Naidu is also well acclaimed for her contribution to poetry. Her poetry had beautiful words that could also be sung. Her collection of poems was published in 1905 under the title "Golden Threshold". She published two other collections called "The Bird of Time", and "The Broken Wings". Later, "The Magic Tree", "The Wizard Mask", and "A Treasury of Poems" were published.

Naidu writes:

Shall hope prevail where clamorous hate is rife,

Shall sweet love prosper or high dreams have place

Amid the tumult of reverberant strife

'Twixt ancient creeds, 'twixt race and ancient race,

That mars the grave, glad purposes of life,

Leaving no refuge save thy succoring face ?

Naidu said, "When there is oppression, the only self-respecting thing is to rise and say this shall cease today, because my right is justice."Naidu adds, "If you are stronger, you have to help the weaker boy or girl both in play and in the work."

In 1916, Naidu published the first biography of Muhammad Ali Jinnah, The Ambassador of Hindu-Muslim Unity.

Kiran Bedi

Kiran Bedi is an Indian police officer and is the first woman to join the Indian Police Service (IPS) in 1972. She was born on 9th June 1949 in Amritsar, Punjab state, India, and is one of the most celebrated and widely known police officers who ever served the Indian Police Force. Kiran Bedi is the second of the four daughters of her parents, Prakash Lal Peshawaria and Prem Lata Peshawaria.

She has been recently appointed as Director General of India's Bureau of Police Research and Development. Earlier, she was Police Advisor in the United Nations peacekeeping department, and has also been honored with the UN medal for outstanding service. In May 2005, she was awarded an honorary degree of Doctor of Law In recognition of her "humanitarian approach to prison reforms and policing".

Education

She completed her schooling from the Sacred Heart Convent School, Amritsar, and obtained her B.A. degree (1964-68) in English from the Government College for Women, Amritsar. She then earned a Master's degree (1968-70) in Political Science from Punjab University, Chandigarh.

Even while in active service in the Indian Police, She continued her educational pursuits, and obtained a Law degree (LLB) in 1988 from Delhi University, Delhi.

She was also awarded a Ph.D. in 1993 in Social Sciences by the Department of Social Sciences, the Indian Institute of Technology, New Delhi. The topic of her thesis was Drug Abuse and Domestic Violence.

Kiran Bedi is also a former all-India and all-Asian tennis champion, and had won the Asian Ladies Title at the age of 22.

Contributions

She began her career as a Lecturer in Political Science (1970-72) at Khalsa College for Women, Amritsar, India. In the year 1972, she was selected for the Indian Police Service. On her web site, she states that she joined the police service "because of my urge to be OUTSTANDING".

She served in a number of tough assignments ranging from Traffic Commissoner of New Delhi, Deputy Inspector General of Police in insurgency prone Mizoram, Advisor to the Lieutanent Governor of Chandigarh, Director General of Narcotics Control Bureau and also on a United Nationsdeputation. She is popularly referred to as Crane Bedi for towing the Prime Minister Indira Gandhi car for parking violation. (the PM was on tour of United States then)

Kiran Bedi influenced several decisions of the Indian Police Service, particularly in the areas of control over narcotics, traffic management, and VIP security. During her stint as the Inspector General of Prisons, Tihar Jail (Delhi), she instituted a number of reforms in the management the prison, and initiated a number of measures such as detoxification programs, yoga, vipassana meditation, and redressing of complaints by prisoners.

Navajyoti (which literally means New Enlightenment), set up in 1988, and India Vision Foundation, set up in 1994, are the two major voluntary organizations established by her with the objectives of improving the condition of the drug addicts and the poor people. Her efforts have won national and international recognition, and her organizations was awarded the Serge Soitiroff Memorial Award for drug abuse prevention by the United Nations.

Awards

Kiran Bedi has received a number of Awards, including the following:

* President's Gallantry Award (1979)
* Women of the Year Award (1980)
* Asia Region Award for Drug Prevention and Control (1991)
* Magsaysay Award (1994) for Government Service
* Mahila Shiromani Award (1995)
* Father Machismo Humanitarian Award (1995)
* Lion of the Year (1995)
* Joseph Beuys Award (1997)
* Pride of India (1999)
* Mother Teresa Memorial National Award for Social Justice (2005)

6

Indian Woman through the Ages

Once the first Prime Minister of India, Jawaharlal Nehru said, "you can tell the condition of a nation by looking at the status of its women". This is absolutely true. Woman of any nation is the mirror to its civilization. If women enjoy good status it shows that the society has reached a level of maturity and sense of responsibility while a decadent image conjures up if the opposite is true. The story of Indian women is as old as the history of Indian civilization.

ANCIENT INDIAN WOMEN

In ancient times Aryans were the main inhabitant of India. These people were mainly Brahmins and they used to give the status of goddess to the women. At that time women enjoyed no less than status of 'Lakshmi' (goddess of wealth) in the households. A famous Sanskrit shloka (form of Hindu verse) signifies the status of women in that era, "Yatra naryastu pujyante, ramante tatra devta" meaning, the place where women are worshipped, god themselves inhabit that place. The women of ancient times had immense power this is evident from a South Indian legend that once a king accidentally killed the husband of a women and she had such powers that she burnt the whole kingdom to ashes. Women in that time had place even superior to men. They had representation in each arena from assemblies to religious rituals. In fact no religious ritual of Hindu Brahmins was supposed to be complete without the presence of the women. An incident of Ramayana is a proof of this as when Lord Rama was performing "Ashvamedha yajna" his wife Sita was not with him and he had to use the gold idol of his wife to compensate for her absence.

Ancient Indian women had say in each and every aspect related to their lives. They had the right to choose their own life partners. The process of choosing the life partner of own choice was known as "Swayamvar" in which grooms assembled at the house of bride and she used to choose the one whom she liked. Maharishi Ved Vyas' Mahabharata and Mahrishi Valmiki's Ramayana bear testimonial to this. In Mahabharata, Draupadi's father arranged for her 'Swanyamvar' and Arjuna (a Pandava prince in exile) successfully managed to fulfill the conditions and became eligible to marry her.

Even the model women of Tretayuga, (second out of four ages of Hindu mythology) "Sita" also had 'Swanyamva' in which kings of different states participated and Lord Rama won her over by breaking the "Shiv Dhanusha". (Hindu God Shiv's bow) Not only just princely women but the common women were also given the same rights. Women were so important that many of the major battles were fought for them. The fiercest battle of ancient India Mahabharata was fought for the honor of Draupadi (wife of Pandavas, ruler of Indraprastha). The Kauravas (ruler of Hastinapur) insulted her in the court and this led to the enmity between cousins and resulted in the most devastating battle of ancient India.

Another example of women power is evident from the cause of death of most learned man of his time Ravana. He was the best scholar of his time and was the master of all the four Vedas of Hindu religion and had immense powers. Even gods were not able to defeat and kill him but a woman was able to bring his doom. Ravana captured Sita and tried to marry her forcibly which led to his destruction.

Women were not just confined to domestic arena but they were also part of religious teachings. In ancient India woman like Gayatri, Maitreyi, Anusuya were renowned seers of their time this shows that women had the right to religious teachings. They were not prohibited even from learning. They could learn whatever they wanted.

The status of women of Vedic era began to decline with time. Gender inequality started creeping into the society. Slowly women's status degraded to such an extent that they were not given the freedom, which was available to even Sudras (lowest caste of ancient Hindu society). They were not given the basic rights. They were debarred from religious practices. They began to lose their political freedom as well. As Vedic age progressed, the status of women became worst. And till the time of 'Smirits' (religious scripture of Hindus) the condition became so bad that women were not allowed free access to education they were given education related to just domestic purposes.

MEDIEVAL INDIAN WOMEN

Medieval India was not women's age it is supposed to be the 'dark age' for them. Medieval India saw many foreign conquests, which resulted in the decline in women's status. When foreign conquerors like Muslims invaded India they brought with them their own culture. For them women was the sole property of her father, brother or husband and she does not have any will of her own. This type of thinking also crept into the minds of Indian people and they also began to treat their own women like this. One more reason for the decline in women's status and freedom was that original Indians wanted to shield their women folk from the barbarous Muslim invaders.

As polygamy was a norm for these invaders they picked up any women they wanted and kept her in their "harems". In order to protect them Indian women started using 'Purdah', (a veil), which covers body. Due to this reason their freedom also became affected. They were not allowed to move freely and this lead to the further deterioration of their status. These problems related with women resulted in changed mindset of people. Now they began to consider a girl as misery and a burden, which has to be shielded from the eyes of intruders and needs extra care. Whereas a boy child will not need such extra care and instead will be helpful as an earning hand. Thus a vicious circle started in which women was at the receiving end. All this gave rise to some new evils such as Child Marriage, Sati, Jauhar and restriction on girl education

Sati: The ritual of dying at the funeral pyre of the husband is known as "Sati" or "Sahagaman". According to some of the Hindu scriptures women dying at the funeral pyre of her husband go straight to heaven so its good to practice this ritual. Initially it was not obligatory for the women but if she practiced such a custom she was highly respected by the society. Sati was considered to be the better option then living as a widow as the plight of widows in Hindu society was even worse. Some of the scriptures like 'Medhatiti' had different views it say that Sati is like committing suicide so one should avoid this.

Jauhar: It is also more or less similar to Sati but it is a mass suicide. Jauhar was prevalent in the Rajput societies. In this custom wives immolated themselves while their husband were still alive. When people of Rajput clan became sure that they were going to die at the hands of their enemy then all the women arrange a large pyre and set themselves afire, while their husband used to fight the last decisive battle known as "Shaka", with the enemy. Thus protecting the sanctity of the women and the whole clan.

Child Marriage: It was a norm in medieval India. Girls were married off at the age of 8-10. They were not allowed access to education and were treated as the material being. The plight of women can be imagined by one of the shloka of Tulsidas where he writes [r1] "Dhol, gawar, shudra, pashu, nari, ye sab tadan ke adhikari". Meaning that animals, illiterates, lower castes and women should be subjected to beating. Thus women were compared with animals and were married off at an early age. The child marriage along with it brought some more problems such as increased birth rate, poor health of women due to repeated child bearing and high mortality rate of women and children.

Restriction on Widow Remarriage: The condition of widows in medieval India was very bad. They were not treated as human beings and were subjected to a lot of restrictions. They were supposed to live pious life after their husband died and were not allowed entry in any celebration. Their presence in any good work was considered to be a bad omen. Sometimes heads of widows were also shaved down. They were not allowed to remarry. Any woman remarrying was looked down by the society. This cruelty on widows was one of the main reasons for the large number of women committing Sati. In medieval India living as a Hindu widow was a sort of a curse.

Purdah System: The veil or the 'Purdah' system was widely prevalent in medieval Indian society. It was used to protect the women folk from the eyes of foreign rulers who invaded India in medieval period. But this system curtailed the freedom of women.

Girl Education: The girls of medieval India and especially Hindu society were not given formal education. They were given education related to household chores. But a famous Indian philosopher 'Vatsyayana' wrote that women were supposed to be perfect in sixty four arts which included cooking, spinning, grinding, knowledge of medicine, recitation and many more.

Though these evils were present in medieval Indian society but they were mainly confined to Hindu society. As compared to Hindu society other societies such as Buddhism, Jainism and Christians were a bit lenient. Women in those societies enjoyed far more freedom.

They had easy access to education and were more liberal in their approach. According to these religions gender was not the issue in attaining salvation. Any person whether a man or a woman is entitled to get the grace of god. During the time of king Ashoka women took part in religious preaching.

According to Hiuen Tsang, the famous traveler of that time, Rajyashri, the sister of Harshavardhana was a distinguished scholar of her time. Another such example is the daughter of king Ashoka, Sanghmitra. She along with her brother Mahendra went to Sri Lanka to preach Buddhism.

The status of women in Southern India was better than the North India. While in Northern India there were not many women administrators, in Southern India we can find some names that made women of that time proud. Priyaketaladevi, queen of Chalukya Vikramaditya ruled three villages. Another women named Jakkiabbe used to rule seventy villages. In South India women had representation in each and every field. Domingo Paes, famous Portuguese traveler testifies to it. He has written in his account that in Vijaynagar kingdom women were present in each and every field.

He says that women could wrestle, blow trumpet and handle sword with equal perfection. Nuniz, another famous traveler to the South also agrees to it and says that women were employed in writing accounts of expenses, recording the affairs of kingdom, which shows that they were educated. There is no evidence of any public school in northern India but according to famous historian Ibn Batuta there were 13 schools for girls and 24 for boys in Honavar. There was one major evil present in South India of medieval time. It was the custom of Devadasis.

Devadasis: It was a custom prevalent in Southern India. In this system girls were dedicated to temples in the name of gods and goddesses. The girls were then onwards known as 'Devadasis' meaning servant of god. These Devadasis were supposed to live the life of celibacy.

All the requirements of Devadasis were fulfilled by the grants given to the temples. In temple they used to spend their time in worship of god and by singing and dancing for the god. Some kings used to invite temple dancers to perform at their court for the pleasure of courtiers and thus some Devadasis converted to Rajadasis (palace dancers) prevalent in some tribes of South India like Yellamma cult.

The plight of women in medieval India and at the starting of modern India can be summed up in the words of great poet Rabindranath Tagore:

> *"O Lord Why have you not given woman the right to conquer her destiny?*
>
> *Why does she have to wait head bowed,*
>
> *By the roadside, Waiting with tired patience,*
>
> *Hoping for a miracle in the morrow?"*

MODERN INDIAN WOMEN

The status of women in modern India is a sort of a paradox. If on one hand she is at the peak of ladder of success, on the other hand she is mutely suffering the violence afflicted on her by her own family members. As compared with past women in modern times have achieved a lot but in reality they have to still travel a long way. Their path is full of roadblocks. The women have left the secured domain of their home and are now in the battlefield of life, fully armored with their talent. They had proven themselves. But in India they are yet to get their dues. The sex ratio of India shows that the Indian society is still prejudiced against female. There are 933 females per thousand males in India according to the census of 2001, which is much below the world average of 990 females. There are many problems which women in India have to go through daily. These problems have become the part and parcel of life of Indian women and some of them have accepted them as their fate.

The main problems of Indian women includes:

Malnutrition

Generally in India, women are the one who eat last and least in the whole family. So they eat whatever is left after men folk are satiated. As a result most of the times their food intake does not contain the nutritional value required in maintaining the healthy body. In villages, sometimes women do not get to eat the whole meal due to poverty. The UNICEF report of 1996 clearly states that the women of South Asia are not given proper care, which results in higher level of malnutrition among the women of South Asia than anywhere else in the world. This nutritional deficiency has two major consequences for women first they become anemic and second they never achieve their full growth, which leads to an unending cycle of undergrowth as malnourished women cannot give birth to a healthy baby.

Poor Health

The malnutrition results in poor health of women. The women of India are prejudiced from the birth itself. They are not breastfed for long. In the want of a son the women wants to get pregnant as soon as possible which decreases the caring period to the girl child whereas the male members get adequate care and nutrition. Women are not given the right to free movement that means that they cannot go anywhere on their own if they want and they have to take the permission of male member of family or have to take them along. This results in decrease in women's visit to doctor and she could not pay attention to her health as a result.

Maternal Mortality

The mortality rate in India is among highest in the world. As females are not given proper attention, which results in the malnutrition and then they are married at an early age which leads to pregnancies at younger age when the body is not ready to bear the burden of a child. All this results in complications, which may lead to gynecological problems, which may become serious with time and may ultimately, lead to death.

Lack of Education

In India women education never got its due share of attention. From the medieval India women were debarred from the educational field. According to medieval perception women need just household education and this perception of medieval India still persists in villages of India even today. Girls are supposed to fulfill domestic duties and education becomes secondary for them whereas it is considered to be important for boys. Although scenario in urban areas has changed a lot and women are opting for higher education but majority of Indian population residing in villages still live in medieval times. The people of villages consider girls to be curse and they do not want to waste money and time on them as they think that women should be wedded off as soon as possible.

The main reason for not sending girls to school is the poor economic condition. Another reason is far off location of schools. In Indian society virginity and purity is given utmost importance during marriage and people are afraid to send their girl child to far off schools were male teacher teach them along with boys.

The lack of education is the root cause for many other problems. An uneducated mother cannot look after her children properly and she is not aware of the deadly diseases and their cure, which leads to the poor health of the children. An uneducated person does not know about hygiene this lack of knowledge of hygiene may lead to poor health of the whole family.

Mistreatment

In India violence against women is a common evil. Not just in remote parts but in cities also women bear the brunt. They are subjected to physical and mental violence. They are the one who work most but are not given their due. The women is not safe anywhere neither at home nor at workplace. Every hour a woman is raped in India and every 93 minutes a woman is burnt to death due to dowry problem. There are many laws such as The Hindu Marriage Act of 1955, The Hindu Succession Act of 1956, The Hindu Widow Remarriage Act of 1856, The Hindu Women Right to Property Act of 1937, The Dowry Prohibition Act of 1961, to protect women and punishment is severe but the conviction rate of crime against women is very low in India.

Overworked

Indian women work more than men of India but their work is hardly recognized as they mainly do unskilled work. Their household chores is never counted as a work, if a woman is working in a field to help her husband it will also be not counted as a work. A study conducted by Mies in 1986 states that in Andhra Pradesh a woman works around 15 hours a day during the agricultural season whereas a male on an average works for around 7-8 hours.

Lack of Power

In India a large percentage of women do not have power. They cannot take decisions independently not even related to their own life. They have to take permission of male members for each and every issue. They don't have any say in important household matters and not in matter of their own marriage.

Marriage

The family mainly fixes the marriages in India. The scenario in villages is very bad. The girl is not consulted but is told to marry a guy whom her family has chosen for him. They are taught to abide by the whims and fancies of their husbands. Going against the wishes of husband is considered to be a sin. In marriage husband always has the upper hand. The groom and his parents show as if they are obliging the girl by marrying her and in return they demand hefty dowry.

Dowry

It's a serious issue. Courts are flooded with cases related to death due to dowry harassment by husband and in laws. In ancient times women were given 'Stridhan' when they departed from the house of their parents. This amount of money was given to her as a gift which she can use on her and her children but her in-laws did not have any right on that amount. This amount was supposed to help the girl in time of need. Slowly this tradition became obligatory and took the form of dowry. Nowadays parents have to give hefty amount in dowry, the in laws of their girl are not concerned whether they can afford it or not. If a girl brings large amount of dowry she is given respect and is treated well in her new home and if she does not bring dowry according to expectations of her in laws then she has to suffer harassment. Due to this evil practice many newly wed women of India have to lose their lives.

Female Infanticide/foeticide

As women were supposed to be and in some areas of India are still considered to be curse by some strata of society their birth was taken as a burden. So in past times they were killed as soon as they were born. In some of the Rajput clans of Rajasthan newly born girl child was dropped in a large bowl of milk and was killed. Today with the help of technology the sex of the unborn baby is determined and if it is a girl child then it is aborted down. In all this procedure women do not have any say they have to do according to the wish of their husbands even if she does not wan to abort she have any choice.

Divorce

The divorce rate in India is not so high compared to western countries but it does not mean that marriages are more successful here. The reason behind low level of divorce rate is that it is looked down by the society. It is regarded as the sign of failure of marriage, especially of women. She is treated as if she has committed some crime by divorcing her husband. In some communities like Muslims women did not have the right to divorce their husband they were divorced at just the pronouncement of " I divorce you" by their husband thrice and they could not do anything except to be the mute spectator. Recently Muslim Law Board has given right of divorce to women. After divorce women is entitled to get her "Mehr" for herself and her children's sustenance. In Hindu society women get maintenance for themselves and their children after divorce.

The statistics testifies to the brutalities afflicted on women folk.

Social Indicator	India	World
Infant Mortality Rate, per 1000 live births	73	60
Maternal Mortality Rate, per 100,000 live births	570	430
Female Literacy, %	58	77.6
Female School Enrollment	47	62
Earned Income by females, %	26	58
Underweight Children, %	53	30
Total Fertility Rate	3.2	2.9
Women in Government, %	6	7
Contraception usage, %	44	56
Low birth weight babies, %	33	17

Though there are problems in the lives of Indian women but they are always ready to fight all the odds and enjoy their life to the full they have their own talent, hobbies, and they socialize according to Indian customs.

Attire

In ancient India both men and women used to wear clothes, which did not need stitching. This custom resulted in women wearing the unstitched long clothe to cover the lower part of body this clothe came to be known as 'Sari' and the upper half of the body was covered with "Stanpatta", modern day 'choli' or blouse which was tied at the back. This attire of the past along with certain modifications continues till today. It is the major attire in rural India. In northern India and especially in cities women also wear 'Salwar kameez', which is comfortable in workplace. Nowadays some women in urban India also wear westernized dresses like trousers and shirts but majority of the women wear Indian attire.

Recreational Activities

Indian women pass her free time with her family or socializing with her friends and husband's family. The major part of housewives time is spent in looking after the family especially children.

Women's Struggle and Reforms

Though women of India are not at par with her counterpart in Western world but she is struggling hard to make her mark in men's world. We can count on certain names from the British India where women put the example of extraordinary bravery which even men might not be able to show. Rani Lakshmi Bai of Jhansi was the one such woman. She was the one who put even British rulers to shame with her extraordinary feats in battle. She fought for her kingdom, which Dalhousie, British Governor General, had unlawfully annexed. She was in a true sense the leader of uprising of 1857. There are certain men who took the cause of women in India. There have been social reformers like Raja Ram Mohan Roy, Ishwar Chandra

Vidyasagar, Swami Vivekanand, Swami Dayananda Saraswati who have helped women gain their previous status in society.

Raja Ram Mohan Roy

Born on 22nd may 1772 he was the torchbearer of social reforms for the women. He was strictly against the evils prevalent in society in his time. He is the one who has done women a great favor by abolishing Sati lawfully. It was due to his efforts that Lord William Bentinck banned the custom of Sati in 1829.

Though this law was not a great deterrent but it changed mindset of people to some extent. Ram Mohan Roy also did great work in the field of women education. He was against child marriage and favored widow remarriage. He himself married a widow thus setting the example for the whole society. Along with 'Dwarka Nath Tagore' he founded "Brahmo Samaj" for the reform of Indian society and emancipation of women.

Ishwar Chandra Vidyasagar

Ishwar Chandra Vidyasagar was popularly known as Vidyasager, which means sea of knowledge. Testifying to his name he was truly the sea of knowledge. He was a pillar of social reform movement of Bengal in 19th century. He widely read ancient Hindu scriptures and came to know that the gender divide which was prevalent in Bengal was not encoded in our ancient texts instead it is the politics to keep women subordinate to men. He strongly supported women education in Bengal and went door to door to persuade people to send their girl child to school. He also did a lot in the field of widow remarriage. He opened many schools for girls.

Mahatma Jyotirao Phule

Born on April 11, 1827, Pune, Jyotirao Govindrao Phule was a real philanthropist. He was the one to open first girl school in India. He is also credited with opening first home for widows of the upper caste and a home for newborn girl children so that they can be saved from female infanticide.

Swami Dayananda Saraswati

He was the founder of Arya Samaj and gave a cry, "back to Vedas". He translated Vedas from Sanskrit to Hindi so that a common man can read it and understand that the Vedic Hindu scriptures gave utmost importance to women. He emphasized for the equal rights for women in every field. He tried to change the mindset of people with his Vedic teachings.

Mahatma Gandhi

The social reformers of 19th century laid down the stage for the emancipation of women but it was Mohan Das Karam Chand Gandhi under whose influence these reforms reached masses[r10]. He was the one who liberated Indian women from the clutches of 'Purdah' and other social evils. He brought them from their confinement and asked them to participate in the struggle for independence.

According to him women should be liberated from the slavery of kitchen only then their true potential could be realized. He said that responsibility of household is important for women but it should not be the only one. In fact she should come forward to share the responsibilities of nation.

When Gandhiji came to the stage of Indian struggle for independence then the average life span of Indian women was 27 years and only 2%women were educated this shows what a Herculean task it was to bring the women of India who was not getting her basic rights to fight for the cause of the nation.

But it was due to his efforts that so many women like Sarojini Naidu, Vijayalakshmi Pandit, Aruna Asaf Ali, Sucheta Kriplani and Rajkumari Amrit Kaur came forward. He spread the message of equality of the gender to the masses and criticized the desire of Indian people to have male child instead of a female.

Gandhiji was strictly against the child marriage and favored widow remarriage. He urged the youth to come forward and accept young widows as their life partner. He said that the girls are also capable of everything boys can do but the need of the time is to give them opportunities so that they can prove themselves. It was mainly due to his efforts that when India got independence 'right to vote' came naturally to Indian women whereas in other developed nations like England and America women got this right very late and that too after lot of protest.

Current Scenario

Some Bright Spots

*India has world's largest number of professionally qualified women.

*India has largest population of working women in the world.

*India has more number of doctors, surgeons, scientists, professors than the United States

Women Achiever with the help of these social reformers women of India slowly started recognizing her true potential. She started questioning the rules laid down for her by the society. As a result, started breaking barriers and earned a respectable position in the world. Today Indian women have excelled in each and every field from social work to visiting space station. There is no arena, which remained unconquered by Indian women. Whether it is politics, sports, entertainment, literature, technology everywhere we can hear applauses for her.

Politics

Women of India are highly active today in this area. Sarojini Naidu, Vijaylakshami Pandit, Sucheta Kriplani were the torchbearer for the women of India. Mrs.Vijay Lkshami Pandit was the first Indian woman to hold a post in the cabinet. Thus paving the way for other women.

The most important name in the category of women politicians of recent times is Mrs Indira Gandhi. She was the one who made world stop and notice the talent and potential of Indian women. She was the first women Prime Minister of independent India. Today her daughter-in law Mrs Sonia Gandhi is following her footsteps and leading the Indian National Congress.

Other women who have made their name in politics of India are Shiela Dixit, Uma Bharti, Jayalalitha, Vasundhra Raje and Mamata Banerjee.

Sports

Indian women have achieved great laurels for the nation in every sport. Whether it is cricket or hockey India have national women team for every game. Indian women cricket team has won Asia Cup of 2004 and 2005 and made country proud. Some women sports icons of India are:

* P.T. Usha (Athletics)
* Kunjarani Devi (Weight lifting)
* Diana Edulji (Cricket)
* Sania Mirza (Tennis)
* Karnam Malleshwari (Weight lifting)

Art and Entertainment

This arena is full of Indian women. We have many names to boast of like M.S. Subbulakshmi, Indian Nightingale Lata Mangeshkar, Asha Bhosle as famous singers. Madhu Bala, Rekha, Aishwarya Rai as Bollywood queens. Today Indian woman is a painter, an actor, a singer, and a beauty queen.

Literature

In past women of India used to write, but their work did not get the recognition. Today they are getting their dues. Arundhati Roy, Anita Desai, Kiran Desai, Shobhaa De, Jhumpa Lahiri are famous names in Indian literature. Not just in India now these women are recognized all over the world. Arundhati Roy has been awarded with the Booker Prize of 1997 for her work "God of Small Things". Kiran Desai has been given Booker Prize of 2006 and Jhumpa Lahiri got recognition in the form of Pulitzer prize.

Corporate Divas

Kiran Majumdar Shaw is the undisputed corporate queen of India. She is the richest Indian woman. She is the MD of Biocon India. She is the wealthiest entrepreneur of India Kiran wanted to become a doctor but could not get admission in medical colleges but even then she did not lose courage and went on to become India's first woman 'Brew Master' and subsequently corporate queen.

Another names in this list include Vidya Mohan Chhabaria, Chairperson of Jumbo Group, Naina Lal Kidwai, Vice Chairperson and Managing Director of HSBC Securities and Capital Market, Sullaijja Firodia Motwani and Mallika Srinivasan.

Social Saints

The Indian saint of today's times Mother Teresa is the name which every Indian whether rich or poor is familiar with. She was the person who used to consider the smile of her countrymen as her wealth.

She worked for those whom even their own families have deserted. She did not care whether she is in the company of a person suffering from communicable disease or whether it is day or night. Whenever or wherever one needed her she was present. She opened various homes for these people most famous of which is 'Nirmal Hriday". It is open to everyone irrespective of caste, creed or religion.

Another important names working for the cause of people includes Aruna Roy who worked for the save RTI Campaign and Medha Patekar who is associated with Narmada Bachao Andolan.

Universal Queens

Indian women have not just made their mark on earth but they have engraved their name in the whole universe by flying to space. Kalpana Chawla, who was the member of Colombia Space Shuttle, which exploded on its way back, was the first Indian women astronaut who visited space station. And now following on her footsteps another women of Indian origin Sunita Williams has become the second one to be the member of International Space Station crew.

Indian women have mastered anything and everything which a woman can dream of. But she still has to go a long way to achieve equal status in the minds of Indian men. The desire of Indian women can be best summed up in the following lines of 'Song of an African Women':

I have only one request.

I do not ask for money

Although I have need of it,

I do not ask for meat...

I have only one request,

And all I ask is

That you remove

The road block

From my path.

7

INDIA: WOMEN'S VOCATIONAL TRAINING

Independent Living is a western concept that has not achieved wide acceptance in developing countries due to its emphasis on individuality and self-sufficiency, and its lack of consideration of family and cultural norms. However, young women with disabilities in many countries are significantly affected by such cultural norms which disadvantage their ability to access vocational training programmes.

This study demonstrates that a culturally appropriate form of Independent Living can be implemented to address this problem. Nine young Indian women with disabilities were interviewed over a two year period while undergoing a training programme in prosthetics and orthotics. Most of the women also lived together during the training. The qualitative analysis demonstrates that women with disabilities may be able to benefit from independent group living as an adjunct to vocational training and can make significant improvements in their personal, social and professional development.

INTRODUCTION

Women with disabilities have been largely neglected when it comes to research, state policies, the disability and women's movements, and rehabilitation programmes, and this has become a widely accepted fact in recent years. Specifically, the lack of vocational training programmes for women with disabilities in developing countries has become a factor contributing to women's continued disadvantage and oppression. Agendas for action arising from major disability and women's conferences in the past decade have all recognised the need for more vocational, training and educational programmes for women with disabilities. However, unequal access to vocational training programmes remains a reality for most women in India, despite the widespread opinion that equal opportunity should exist.

The inability of Indian women with disabilities to access vocational training programmes is not always a simple reflection of a lack of programmes. In many cases, women cannot participate because of structural and societal barriers resulting from factors related to gender, class and disability. Boylan identified several such barriers to disabled women's participation in rehabilitation services which included: poverty, rural isolation from services, inaccessible buildings and transportation to services, parental overprotection, and low self-esteem. Kern argues that even when women with disabilities are able to participate, vocational training programmes tend to be male-dominated and do not provide women with adequate social support.

As a result, many women are compelled to leave the programmes before they are completed. Kern advocates for training and rehabilitation programmes in which sufficient numbers of women participate, to ensure the social and moral support required to build their self-confidence. She insists that these programmes recognise the barriers specific to women with disabilities, and that they implement strategies that facilitate women's full participation.

This chapter examines independent group living as a strategy that can facilitate women's access to vocational training programmes. More specifically, it examines independent group living as an arrangement that can provide women with the support required to develop at the personal and social levels, thus enhancing their self-esteem, independence, and motivation to succeed in training and future employment.

METHOD

The opportunity to live independently of their families, and as a group, was an experimental arrangement offered by the

Association of People with Disability (APD) and Mobility India (MI) in Bangalore, India.

It was a key strategy to ensure that poor, rural women with disabilities could access a training programme that would teach them prosthetic and orthotic manufacturing skills for two years, and help them set up a co-operative mobility aids workshop in the third year. A small house was rented near APD's Orthotic Centre, and women enrolled in the programme were encouraged to reside there.

The women received monthly stipends which covered the rent costs. It was recognised that the provision of this living arrangement was necessary if the women were to transcend their barriers of poverty, rural isolation, and the difficulties (both financial and physical) of daily travel to and from the centre. Without the opportunity to live independently and at no cost, these women would not have been able to access the training programme due to the distant location of their family homes and the poor financial situations of their families.

Further, living as a group was considered the most viable arrangement due to the women's gender. It was understood that the women would face considerable opposition from their families if they resided alone in the city, and that they would not feel safe or comfortable doing so. This initiative was therefore attentive to the multiple issues facing these women, such as rural location, class, gender, and parental overprotection. Independent group living was a strategy intended to assist in gaining family permissions for training, to provide social support to the women, and to be a safer and more economical arrangement than living alone or travelling long distances from family homes.

A study was conducted in 1996 and 1997 to examine the effects of independent living on this group of young Indian women with disabilities. Individual and group interviews were conducted with the nine women over the two-year programme. The focus of the study was to examine independent group living as an arrangement for enhancing women's development at the individual and social levels, while simultaneously providing them with the support and confidence needed to maintain access to vocational training. The results presented here describe the key areas of development that resulted from independent group living:

1. Development of independent living skills;
2. Social Development (increased sociability, public confidence and ability to support others) and
3. Personal Development (improved self-image, independence and professional motivation).

RESULTS AND DISCUSSION

Independent Living Skills

In total, there were nine young women engaged in the orthotics and prosthetics training programme. Three of these women lived in their parents or relatives' homes for the duration of the programme, because their houses were in close proximity to the training centre in Bangalore. It was possible, then, to draw certain conclusions about the differences in levels of development between the six women who lived independently in the group house and those that remained with their families. It became evident, for example, that the women living as a group developed practical and independent living skills in ways that were not possible for the others.

Upon joining the programme, most of the women reported that their parents were overprotective and did not think them capable or expect them to do household chores: "Even coffee she (mother) brings it wherever I am. I am not allowed to remove the lunch plate. By chance if I removed the plate my father used to scold my brothers' wives. 'Her leg is not all right, why do you allow her to do that? What is wrong with you people?' My brothers and my father used to scold them saying, 'Don't make that child do things.'"

Living in the group house, the women were able to share the skills they had with each other, and learn many things that would not have been possible had they remained with their families. They invented several systems that facilitated their ability as a group to live independently and comfortably. For example, they began a routine of cooking in pairs, so that the women who did not know how to cook could learn from those who had experience. For chores involving heavy labour, such as carrying water, they all participated in completing the task: "There is a tap next to our room. Rajni, Mira, and Rajasri cannot get water from that tap. But Namita is okay. Mohua also can lift. Only I can lift alone. Mohua will lift the water, give it to Namita, and she gives it to me and I carry it."

The women also developed money-management skills. They organised a "mess-system" in which they each contributed 300 rupees of their stipend each month, and then collaborated on which foods to buy. With these funds, the women went to the market and purchased food sufficient to last for a month-a responsibility that would have been impossible had they lived at home: "We ourselves do the work, we ourselves go for purchases. How much money we save, how much is spent we learn. All this we like. Because at home our parents will take care of everything. We don't know at all. Which item is costly, which item is cheaper..."

In sum, living independently of their families gave the young women a chance to run a household and learn such tasks as cooking, cleaning, and money-management. These skills gave the women self-confidence, and helped prepare them for a future in which they would need to live independently to continue their work in the city.

SOCIAL DEVELOPMENT

Increased Sociability and Confidence

Women with disabilities, especially from rural areas, are likely to be left out of family interactions and community activities. In addition, they are exposed to social stigma and stereotyping within their communities, which leads them to feel devalued, isolated, and ashamed. Among the women in this study, all but one had felt embarrassed, isolated and alone at social functions, festivals, or when people came to their family's houses to visit: "Since I was young I never used to go out. I never attended marriages. I used to feel shy because I am handicapped. In my house I am the only one who is like this and I used to feel very bad."

The experience of independent group living seemed to have a beneficial impact on the women's levels of sociability and their confidence to venture out in public or to social functions. Living among other women with disabilities and in a non-judgemental environment was of great benefit in raising self-esteem and in developing social skills. All of the women who resided in the group house reported feeling accepted, sociable, and confident to venture into town. Because they went on social outings as a group, they did not feel isolated or personally affronted if someone stared at them. Together, confidence in their abilities was strengthened and they could carry out their business with mutual support.

This social support also gave the women confidence to be more sociable and extroverted when they were visiting their families: "My mother says, 'I had never thought you would live independently and boldly'. Before I was very shy. I never used to stay alone. When there were visitors I used to go inside and sit. I never used to talk to anybody and got scared easily. When I wanted to go outside I used to take my mother or father... Now I go everywhere independently."

It is important to note that those women who lived with their families or relatives during the training programme did not notice any significant changes in their levels of sociability. Although they reported feeling more accepted and talkative while at work, they continued to feel isolated and stigmatised in their communities after work. The women who lived as a group, however, felt accepted, confident and sociable on a more constant basis.

MUTUAL SUPPORT AND TAKING ON CARING ROLES

From childhood on, many women with disabilities are regarded as social and economic burdens by their families and communities. Boyce and Pruthvish state that discrimination based on gender and disability decreases disabled women's chances of marriage, having children, or earning a living. Women with disabilities are deprived of their traditional roles and status as wives and mothers, and often feel emotionally unfilled and inferior to other women as a result. Some women with disabilities often lead lives of total dependence-both emotionally and financially-and never have the chance to provide care for themselves or for others

Opportunities to fulfil caring roles arose immediately for the six women upon moving into their group house. The women reported that they missed their families deeply and provided each other with emotional support through this period. As time went on, they reported that this atmosphere of mutual caring and support allowed them to adjust to being separated from their families. The women cared for each other in many ways, both emotionally and physically, through their stay in the house.

In addition to taking on the roles of caregivers within the group house, all six of the women concluded that they would provide for their parents in the future. Confidence in their ability to provide and care for others was so strong that, in several cases, they came to see themselves as being more responsible for maintaining their parents' well-being than their brothers and sisters. One woman said:

> *"I have this desire to tell her (mother) not to go to anyone, not even to my younger brother...I told mother, 'I won't leave you in anybody's house. I want to earn money myself and keep you. You should not have any difficulties'."*

The other women reported similar sentiments, and expressed the desire to rent houses and bring their mothers to Bangalore after the orthotics workshop was underway. Thus, the women's perceptions of themselves in relation to their families developed significantly during the two-year training period. They went from feeling completely dependent on their parents for economic, emotional, and physical security, to feeling that they could provide support and security to their parents in the future.

PERSONAL DEVELOPMENT

Improved Self-Image: Attitudes towards Disability, Marriage and Gender

The women's attitudes towards their own disabilities improved dramatically as they spent more time around others like themselves. There were two aspects to this development. First, the women reported that after working with clients at the orthotic centre they no longer felt powerless or disadvantaged by their disabilities. In fact, all women in the training (both those living in the group house and those living with their families) said that they now felt privileged in relation to others with disabilities. The women's acknowledgement of their relative privilege contributed to an enhanced self-image and also motivated them to continue training as orthotic technicians.

Second, the experience of independent group living enhanced the women's self-image with regard to their disabilities. As mentioned earlier, the three women who remained with their families during the training programme felt isolated and stigmatised when they returned home in the evenings. The women who stayed in the group house, however, did not feel alone with their disabilities, and expressed that they now felt as capable and normal as anyone else: "At home I used to think among so many brothers and sisters, I am alone like this. After coming here, I realised that I need not sit in a wheelchair, I need not sit at home. At least I have legs to walk. I have some strength in my hands and legs, I can work. Thinking this I have hope to further improve. Now I don't think that I have a disability."

It is evident that the women's attitudes towards their disabilities became increasingly positive as they spent time among their co-workers and other people with disabilities who came to the orthotic centre. The experience of independent group living, however, also facilitated an improved self-image on a constant basis.

Likewise, the women's attitudes towards marriage and their options for the future became more defined and opinionated as time went on. The experience of being self-sufficient-both at work and in the group household-caused the women to value their ability to self-determine their lives.

They came to value their freedom and independence, and many were unwilling to have this taken away by a husband: "If someone asks (me to marry him) I will say no. I want to be with mother till the end...I will be fine, enjoying and free. I can eat when I want, do what I want, watch TV. Marriage means I have to look after all different people...Now, I just keep my bag on the table and sleep. Can I do that after marriage? Not possible. We won't have so much freedom."

The women also developed an awareness of the gender dynamics involved in marriage, and about how these dynamics could intensify if a woman was disabled. They were aware of the expected work roles in the family, in that the male would expect to be the breadwinner and the female would be expected to stay home.

After living independently and working in the orthotic centre, however, the women said that they would only marry if they knew they would be able to continue working and earning their own wages.

The women also became aware that disabled women were at higher risk for abuse in marriage. They made many references to able-bodied women who were being abused by their husbands, and expressed fear that their disabilities would heighten their chance of being mistreated by their husbands. The women expressed an unwillingness to expose themselves to such abuse, regardless of the status and security that marriage could bring.

In sum, living and working independently gave the women increased self-confidence in their ability to survive without being married. This was a very important development, because many of the women reported that they used to feel depressed about their low prospects of finding a husband. Now, they felt happy and self-sufficient, and reported that they would never sacrifice their new-found independence, even if they had the chance to marry.

PROFESSIONAL INTEREST AND MOTIVATION

All of the trainees excelled in the two-year programme, learning technical skills, patient-care skills, and the business and organisational skills necessary to successfully run an independent workshop. However, the opportunity to learn skills and find future economic independence is not always enough to motivate women to complete vocational training programmes. Women with disabilities often abandon their training before it is completed, because of unwelcome and non-supportive social environments and male-domination in training centres (5). Of interest then, is how the experience of independent group living while in training affected the women's interest and motivational levels with regard to the programme and their future careers.

The study found that the women's attitudes towards work and training underwent significant change over the course of the programme. The women had, for the most part, joined the training in pursuit of employment that would help themselves and their families financially. Although they initially exhibited some interest in the idea of doing prosthetic and orthotic work, they were relieved at that point to find any employment.

After the training was underway, however, there was a growing belief amongst the women that their work was socially valuable and necessary for the well-being of persons with disabilities. This sense of inspiration and moral obligation to help others developed because of the women's experiences while at work, both by seeing how their work was directly helping others and by becoming aware of the great need that existed for their services.

Of significance is that the six women residing in the group house reported that they would not leave the training programme or the orthotics workshop even if they were offered a job with a better salary. The three other trainees, who lived with their families during the course of the training, reported that they would indeed quit the training if offered a better salary. In the end, two of these trainees did quit the programme.

In addition, the women who lived as a group reported that their ability to learn was facilitated by the fact that each evening they did their homework together, and discussed the events of the day. In contrast, the women living with their families reported that it was difficult to keep up with their homework because of family interruptions, lack of family support or interest, and other dynamics in their households.

It is possible that the three women living outside the group house had a lower commitment to their training and work because they felt less committed to the other women in the programme. For the other six women, the experience of living as a group resulted in high group cohesion, strong friendships, and emotional commitment to one another. Leaving the training programme did not seem like an option for the women who lived independently, because they were as committed to each other as they were to their new profession. In sum, independent group living provided the women with a support system that allowed them to maintain interest, motivation and excitement about their training and their futures as orthotic and prosthetic technicians. In August 1997, the seven remaining women completed their training and received their certificates as prosthetic and orthotic technicians. Shortly thereafter, the co-operative workshop was formally inaugurated, and it is still operating today.

CONCLUSION

The study has shown that the success of this particular group of women was linked as much to the experience of independent group living as to the vocational training opportunity itself. All six women who lived independently as a group completed the training and went on to run their own self-supporting business. Only one of the three women who lived with her family during the training accomplished this feat. Independent group living allowed the women to develop in ways that would not have been possible had they remained with their families, and the benefits were many.

First, the opportunity to live as a group within the city clearly gave the women access to the programme. Without this option, these women would not have been able (physically or financially) to travel each day to the vocational training centre. Independent group living was therefore a successful strategy put forth by these organisations to facilitate poor, rural disabled women's basic access to training opportunities.

Second, the women learned independent living skills on a practical level, acquiring experience in household management and self-care that will benefit them for the rest of their lives. Living independently as a group gave them the confidence they needed to live without their parents in the city and to pursue their professional interests following the training program.

Third, the experience of living amongst other women with disabilities benefited the women's social development. The social support and mutual caring that developed in the group house enhanced the women's self-esteem and confidence in terms of sociability and courage to interact with the general public. The social skills and public confidence they acquired living as a group may benefit them for the rest of their lives, especially in terms of succeeding in business within the city. In addition, the women were able to take on caring roles, providing emotional and physical support to others in ways that they had never permitted in their family homes. This new role benefited them in terms of emotional fulfilment, and also allowed them to explore the idea of providing for their parents in old age. This confidence to care for themselves and for others was a remarkable development considering that they had spent most of their lives depending on others.

Finally, the women experienced major growth at the personal level. Their self-images improved drastically, both with regard to their disabilities and in their attitudes towards marriage and the future. Living independently during the two-year training programme showed them that they were relatively privileged in relation to many others with disabilities. Consequently they could succeed in a household or working environment despite their disabilities, and they also could be self-sufficient and happy without being married. Further, the experience of living as a group contributed to enhanced motivation and professional interest among the six women, due to high group cohesion and the social support that such a living situation provided. In sum, the benefits of independent group living during this training initiative were immense.

Independent living, as a concept, originated in the western world to improve the lives of persons with disabilities. However, independent living has been criticised in the developing world for its focus on individualism over communalism and its apparent rejection of family interdependence and cultural tradition. This study demonstrates that the basic benefits of independent living, an increase in self-esteem and social integration, can be achieved with a uniquely eastern approach that also respects cultural norms and values.

Indeed the definition of Independent Living that was adopted by the Asia Pacific Regional Conference of Rehabilitation International in 1995 is applicable to the APD experiment: "Independent living means living just like everyone else-having opportunities to make decisions that affect one's life, being able to pursue activities of one's own choosing-limited only in the same ways that one's non-disabled neighbours are limited. Independent living should not be defined in terms of living on one's own. Independent living has to do with self-determination. And, it is having the freedom to fail-and to learn from one's failures-just as non-disabled people do."

The provision of financially-supported group living arrangements is strongly recommended for future vocational training initiatives of this type, in order to combat the barriers of class, disability, gender, and rural poverty experienced by many women with disabilities.

8

Stabilizing Population

Every ten years, since 1974, the world community religiously assembles to review the status of population growth, its distribution and movement at the global level. Most of us are well aware why there is great concern about the population explosion and its consequences. It is said, Asia accounts for 60% of the total world's population, while India alone contributes about 16%.

It is heartening to note that there is a paradigm shift with regard to population growth and how to bring it down, particularly after the Conference on Population held at Cairo in 1994. Very few people talk about population as a problem in the traditional demographic sense. Population experts are now portraying the population scenario in the broader context of development.

They all have called for policy action based on the unmet needs and desires of men, women and families as well. However, despite their attempts and endeavours, the rates of population increase remain quite high in many parts of the globe. This calls for a critical reflection on what might be the best possible approach to the population explosion syndrome that we are experiencing today, particularly in India.

In 1952, India was the first country in the world to launch a national programme, emphasizing family planning to the extent necessary for reducing birth rates "to stabilize the population at a level consistent with the requirement of national economy". After 1952, sharp declines in death rates were however, not accompanied by a similar drop in birth rates. The National Health Policy, 1983 stated that replacement levels of total fertility rate, TFR (the average number of children born to a woman during her lifetime) should be achieved by the year 2000.

ONE BILLION ON 11TH MAY

On 11 May 2000 India is projected to have 1 billion (100 crore) people, i.e., 16 per cent of the world's population on 2.4 per cent of the globe's land area. If current trends continue, India may overtake China in 2045, to become the most populous country in the world. While global population has increased threefold during this century, from 2 billion to 6 billion, the population of India has increased nearly five times from 238 million (23 crore) to 1 billion in the same period. India's current annual increase in population of 15.5 million is large enough to neutralize efforts to conserve the resource endowment and environment.

The population of India has been estimated at 970.9 million as on 1 July 1998 showing an increase of more than 124.6 million since the last census conducted in 1991(846.3 million). In 1947, when India attained Independence, the population of India was estimated to be around 342 million. As per the estimates of Sample Registration System of the office of the Registrar General of India, the population of India is increasing at a rate of 15.5 million per year.

In other words, the last 100 million has been added in less than six years. It may be recalled that before Independence, it took 42 years to add 100 million. Since 1951, when the first Census in independent India was conducted, about 600 million have been added to the population of India. The first 100 million was added in 12.5 years, the second 100 million in 9.3 years, the third 100 million in 6.4 years, the fifth and sixth 100 million in 5.8 years.

It has been estimated by the Technical Working Group on Population Projections appointed by Planning Commission that by 2016 India's population would go up to 1263 million, i.e., by another 31%. While the population of states of Kerala, Orissa and Tamil Nadu will increase by 15% to 19% during 1998-2016, in the states of Bihar, Madhya Pradesh, Rajasthan and Uttar Pradesh it would increase by over 40%, the highest anticipated increase being in Uttar Pradesh with 55%. UP's population will cross a mind-boggling figure of 242.8 million by 2016.

GROWING PRESSURE IN URBAN AREAS

The urban population of India has been estimated at 268.8 million as on 1 March 1998. The 1991 census figure was 217.2 million. It has been projected to increase to 425 million in 2016 or an increase of 208 million during a period of 25 years 1991-2016. In other words the urban population would almost double in 25 years.

The annual addition to urban population would be around 8.05 million. This would put a severe constraint on infrastructure facilities such as housing, water supply, sanitation and transportation. Around 2/3 of this urban population lived in about 132 class-I cities with a population of 1,00,000 and above in 1991.

In recent years the realization has grown that people are the real wealth of a nation. Progress of a country is measured not only in terms of income expansion and commodity production but also in terms of expansion of human capabilities. Even though countries with higher average income tend to have higher life expectancies, lower infant mortality rates and higher literacy rates, these associations are far from perfect. Inter-country comparisons of income variations tend to explain less than half the variations in life expectancy or infant mortality rate.

This does not mean that economic growth is not essential for improving quality of life. How the different segments of the population share the fruits of economic growth are equally important to consider. In particular what the poor get and how much additional resources are used to support public services such as primary health care and basic education are important to consider.

EXPECTATION OF LIFE AT BIRTH

At the time of Independence, expectations of life at birth for the country as a whole was around 32 years. This has increased to 60.3 years during 1991-95. The figures for males and females were 59.7 and 60.9 respectively. The corresponding figures during 1941-51, centred around 1946 were 32.5 and 31.7 years.

INFANT MORTALITY

At the time of Independence the infant mortality was estimated to be around 180 per 1000 live births. This has decreased by more than half to 74 in 1995.

EDUCATION

The percentage of literate population aged 7 and above has increased from 18.3 in 1951 to 52.2 in 1991. The corresponding figures for males and females were 27.2 and 8.9 in 1951 and 64.7 and 39.2 in 1991. According to National Sample Survey Organisation (NSSO) survey 1997, the literacy percentage in the country stands at 62. The NSSO figure show that in the current decade, in a matter of just six years, the decadal average of all earlier years has been surpassed.

GENDER JUSTICE AND EMPOWERMENT

Of late "Gender Justice" and "Women Empowerment" have received adequate attention of the governments of developed as well as developing nations. However, the debate on gender development and population planning has received attention only after the United Nation's International Conference on Population held at Cairo in 1994; International Conference on Women held at Beijing in 1995; and Social Summit Conference held at Copenhagen, in 1995. Moreover, UNDP's Human Development Reports 1995 and 1996 have also laid emphasis on Women and development.

The gender issues have emerged due to the fact that while sex is biologically determined the gender and its role specifications are socially, culturally, and traditionally and to some extent religiously constructed. The patriarchal norms dominate society and therefore most women experience "gender oppression" to a greater or lower degree.

The status of women in India is also very low. Out of India's total work force of 314 million, 90 million are women. Figures based on 1991 census and the National Sample Survey Organisation show that 86.5 per cent of women are employed in rural areas. Among rural women workers, 87 per cent of women workers are employed in unorganized sectors like household industries, petty trades and services, building construction, etc. Further a colossal 70 per cent of them are illiterate. Moreover the health status of the majority of women is not sound and they are also not sufficiently involved in the decision making process.

The Government of India is determined to place adequate emphasis on raising the status of women. The Constitution ensures equality and protection to women citizens. Further, article 610A envisages that it is the constitutional duty of every citizen to renounce practices derogatory to the dignity of women. Since the seventies, the objectives of raising the status of women have also been included in different five-year plans. Moreover, the political empowerment of women by making reservation of seats in panchayat raj system; formulation of National Commission on Women and the draft National Policy on Empowerment of Women which seek to provide justice, equal opportunity for power-sharing and decision-making to women at all levels, are significant steps in this direction.

FAMILY PLANNING

Family Planning Programme in India started way back in 1951 with a clinic-based approach. In the Third Five-Year Plan, Extension Education Programme was adopted with a view to teaching the virtues of a small family. Later came the intra-uterine contraceptive approach was initiated.

All these approaches could not show encouraging results. The new approach which started from 1 April 1996 focussing on improving reproductive and child health care facilities and discarding the earlier target-oriented approach, has given a new lease of life to the family planning endeavours.

Women are the major targets of family planning programmes. According to the National Family Health Survey conducted in India the most widely used method of family planning is female sterilization, which is accepted by 67 per cent of current users as against male sterilization of 3 per cent. This signified that family planning programme has largely remained a women-centred programme. Reluctance of men to use permanent methods, frequent fertility, etc., compel women to accept family planning methods. In many cases their feeble health conditions together with the adoption of family planning methods have eroded their health.

The lack of quick referral services by the family planning service-providers made women to carry the physical and psychological trauma arising out of sterilization and Intra-uterine Device (IUD) insertion. Further, in some cases they have also to bear the ire of husbands, in-laws and even the society in case of conception arising out of failure of vasectomy. Customarily, women are neglected and also in many cases denied of their own reproductive health rights. The condition of illiterate women belonging to lower castes, classes and religiously orthodox communities and in rural areas is more precarious.

MATERNAL MORTALITY

Abortion plays an important role in checking unwanted pregnancies. However, the abortion-related mortality and morbidity in India continue to be high and at least 10 per cent of all maternal death results from abortion. The UNICEF (1990) estimated that roughly five million abortions are performed annually in India and the majority, about 4.5 million are illegal.

Notwithstanding the fact that abortion has been legalized in India since 1972 and the country has one of the least restrictive abortion laws, the existence of widespread illegal and unscientific practices is highly disconcerting. In rural areas, due to socio-cultural bindings precondition of conducting medical termination of pregnancy (MTP) against sterilization in government hospitals, exorbitant charges for MTP by private nursing homes and hospitals, etc., compel impoverished rural people to go in for illegal methods.

However, stigma of pre-marital pregnancies and hiding of unwanted pregnancies by married women has also promoted illegal and unscientific abortion. The unscientific and traditional methods of abortion such as prolapsy, advising pregnant mothers to consume herbs, pressing foetus and other local practices adopted by charlatans, cause a lot of damage to the maternal health in general and reproductive health in particular. Illegal and unscientific abortions and its related morbidity and mortality are the glorious examples of "gender injustice" or "gender oppression".

Maternal death is defined by the World Health Organisation as the death of a woman while pregnant or within 42 days of the termination of pregnancy, irrespective of the duration and the site of pregnancy, from any cause related to or aggravated by pregnancy or its management but not from accidental or incidental causes.

Maternal Mortality Ratio (MMR) i.e., death per 100,000 live births for the early 1990s, as revealed by UNICEF and WHO data, varies from country to country from a high of 1800 in Sierra Leone to a low of 3 in Greece. India stands at 570 and figures for some rural areas are as high as 1000 or 1200. Further, it is estimated that a woman in India faces a 1 in 37 chance of maternal death during her lifetime.

In patriarchal societies such as India, the low status of women contributes to the invisibility and low public importance of maternal mortality. A maternal death is seen as an individual misfortune rather than an event that deserves public concern. Thus these incidents remains private and invisible.

The low sex-ratio, low literacy rate, low participation in legislative, executive and judiciary process, economic dependence and low nutrition and health status are a few indicators which characterize the low status of women in India. In the UN's Human Development Report 1995 India ranks 99th on the

Gender Related Development Index of 130 nations. The Gender Empowerment Measure which estimates the extent of women's participation in a country's economic and political activities, ranks India 110th out of 116 nations. The Report has identified three critical areas, i.e., access to education, reproductive health and credit resources, where women face barriers and therefore, urged that as long as these barriers persist, women will not have equal access to opportunities and to the benefits of development.

Indian development planning has always aimed at removing inequalities in the process of development, recognizing the fact that women lag behind due to several socio-economic-cultural-political impediments. The five-year plans have been paying special attention to women's welfare emphasizing female education access to resources and their political empowerment. Women's empowerment received a fresh impetus in the 1980s when women were recognized as a separate target group in the Sixth Five-Year Plan. Efforts, since then, have been directed towards mainstreaming women into the national development process by raising their overall status--social, economic, legal and political--at par with that of men.

The Central Social Welfare Board in cooperation with NGOs has been conducting awareness generation camps for rural and poor women since 1987-88. It aims at generating awareness of their status in the family and society, their social rights, community health and hygiene, technology and environment, etc.

India has taken some laudable steps to correct the maladies afflicting women and the girl child. As a signatory to the World Declaration on the Survival, Protection and Development of Children, the Government of India has drawn up an Action Plan for the Girl Child (1991-2000). In order to highlight the importance of girl child it has taken the help of media and NGOs for a massive campaign. Further, the Government has now regularized the sex determination test to prevent female foeticide by enacting Pre-Natal Diagnostic Techniques (Regulation and Prevention of Misuse) Act, 1994, which came into force from 1 January 1996.

Coming to the arena of education, the Indian State is obliged to provide for free and compulsory education for women and children as laid down in the Constitution of India--Articles 15(3), 45,46. In line with such objectives, Operation Blackboard scheme was launched in 1987 under the National Policy on Education (NPE), 1986. Similarly, in 1989 a national open schooling system was set up to offer a flexible life-oriented programme through distance education.

Further, the innovative District Primary Education Programme was initiated based on NPE-1986 and Programme of Action-1992, to achieve universalisation of primary education. To make these programmes effective the Government transferred 'education' to the panchayats by the 73rd Amendment Act. The mid-day meal scheme, which was introduced in 1995 to popularize primary education, was again underlined in the conference of Chief Ministers held in New Delhi in July 1996.

During the past fifty years the strategy for women's economic uplift has kept changing from time to time based upon the experiences gained. In the 1990s the strategy has shifted to "empowerment of women" and "giving them a voice" from the earlier welfare and developmental approaches.

The programme for Development of Women and Children in Rural Areas (DWCRA) launched in 1982-83 has received a boost by the addition of two new components--Community-Based Convergent Services (CBCS) and Information, Education and Communication (IEC). Formation of Thrift and Credit Groups of women for self-help and economic self-reliance has also been encouraged by the Government. A Rashtriya Mahila Kosh was set up in 1993 for extending credit with low transaction costs to poor and needy women. The Indira Mahila Yojana launched in 1995 aims at, inter alia, increasing women's awareness and income through group activities. Another scheme, Mahila Samriddhi Yojana for the uplift of rural women, has been operating from 1 October 1993.

For improving the nutrition and health status of women and children, the Government's initiatives so far are encouraging. As emphasized by the World Bank document, "Improving Women's Health in India", reproductive health is one of the keys to curbing population.

CHILD SURVIVAL AND SAFE MOTHERHOOD

A specific Child Survival and Safe Motherhood (CSSM) programme which was launched in 1992-93 with the financial assistance of World Bank and UNICEF, ensures effective ante-natal care, safe delivery, immunization of mother and infant, control of diarrhoeal diseases and respiratory infections, nutritional education and provision of basic medical care.

In addition, the following specific programmes have been under implementation as 100 per cent centrally sponsored scheme:

(i) Universal Immunization Programme (UIP) initiated in 1985 aims at controlling six vaccine preventable diseases--Neonatal tetanus, Diphtheria, Pertussis (whooping cough), Poliomyelitis, Tuberculosis (child) and Measles;

(ii) Oral Rehydration Therapy (ORT) started in 1986-87 aims at preventing deaths due to dehydration among children under 5 years of age;

(iii) Prophylaxis schemes against nutritional anaemia among pregnant and lactating mother and against blindness due to vitamin A deficiency among children;

(iv) The Acute Respiratory Infections control strategy initiated during 1989 for arresting the rate of deaths due to Pneumonia. Several other schemes such as 'dai' (midwife) training programmes, obstetric care programmes, special check ups for primary school children etc., are being implemented.

In 1997, though, a crucial attitudinal shift occurred; from a contraceptive and sterilization-driven programme to a more sensible reproductive and child health scheme. This took into account management of unwanted pregnancy, promotion of safe motherhood and child survival, prevention and management of reproductive tract and sexually transmitted infections, and reproductive health services for adolescents. This approach advocates education and woman's empowerment as a long-term strategy to stabilize population.

STD AND AIDS

The HIV, AIDS and STD epidemics are nowadays affecting all aspects--economic, social, and cultural--of people's lives. Lack of education and reluctance of clients of use condoms are largely responsible for the spread of these diseases. The World Health Organisation has remarked that women in India suffer double the disease burden than men do from sexually transmitted diseases. The National Family Health Survey has pointed out that in most states a large majority of married women have never heard of STD and AIDS. In addition, women who have heard of AIDS harbour a large number of misconceptions about how the disease is transmitted.

Therefore for safe abortion and safe sex, reproductive health education to women and adolescence education to girls should be given. It is suggested that the medical termination of pregnancy facility by lady doctors and counselling and education on AIDS and STD require to be made available and given at the Primary Health Care Centre level.

NATIONAL POPULATION POLICY 2000

The immediate objective of the National Population Policy 2000 is to address the unmet needs for contraception, health care infrastructure, and health personnel, and to provide integrated service delivery for basic reproductive and child health care. The medium term objective is to bring the TFR to replacement levels by 2010, through vigorous implementation of inter-sectoral operational strategies. The long-term objective is to achieve a stable population by 2045, at a level consistent with the requirements of sustainable economic growth, social development, and environmental protection.

In pursuance of these objectives, the following National Socio-Demographic Goals to be achieved in each case by 2010 are formulated:

1. Address the unmet needs for basic reproductive and child health services, supplies and infrastructure.
2. Make school education up to age 14 free and compulsory, and reduce dropouts at primary and secondary school levels to below 20 per cent for both boys and girls.
3. Reduce infant mortality rate to below 30 per 1000 live births.
4. Reduce maternal mortality ratio to below 100 per 100,000 live births.
5. Achieve universal immunization of children against all vaccine preventable diseases.
6. Promote delayed marriage for girls, not earlier than age 18 and preferably after 20 years of age.
7. Achieve 80 per cent institutional deliveries and 100 per cent deliveries by trained persons.
8. Achieve universal access to information/counselling, and services for fertility regulation and contraception with a wide basket of choices.
9. Achieve 100 per cent registration of births, deaths, marriage and pregnancy.
10. Contain the spread of Acquired Immunodeficiency Syndrome (AIDS), and promote greater integration between the management of reproductive tract infections (RTI) and sexually transmitted infections (STI) and the National AIDS Control Organisation.
11. Prevent and control communicable diseases.
12. Integrate Indian Systems of Medicine (ISM) in the provision of reproductive and child health services, and in reaching out to households.
13. Promote vigorously the small family norm to achieve replacement levels of TFR.
14. Bring about convergence in implementation of related social sector programmes so that family welfare becomes a people-centred programme.

It may be the quest for the so-called holistic approach to population containment which is reflected in the list of 14 goals in the new policy or it can be the plain realization that it is an agenda of human development which is focussed on women and children which constitutes the most practical manifestation of a population policy.

Of the 14 goals specified in the Policy 2000, one relates to the long-neglected imperative of free and compulsory school education along with that of reducing the school dropout ratio. Few others relate to the area of health and in particular to the need to reduce the infant mortality rate (IMR) and the maternal mortality ratio besides the universalization of immunization of children against all vaccine-preventable diseases.

The key objective of the Policy 2000 is to bring the fertility rate to "replacement" levels by 2010 and the long-term goal will be to achieve a stable population by the year 2045. The Union Cabinet endorsed the policy and accepted a system of incentives for couples adopting the small family norm, opting to do away with disincentives.

It remains to be seen if this exercise will achieve the desired results, because, given the illiteracy, unless the people see the disincentives for large families, they may not be inclined to stop with two children. The core of the population problem in the country centres on the higher fertility rate among the poorer sections and the explosion taking place in the less developed States.

CONCLUSION

The tyranny of numbers is crushing. Despite rapid strides in agriculture, India's food security is tenuous. The ideal diet is 400 kg per person per year, so experts say India needs to produce at least 300 kg per person per year to be free from the hunger trap.

There are other problems. For one, our total annual requirement of fresh water resources is expected to increase to 1,050 cubic km by 2025; aggravated by pollution, the spectre of water famine stares at us.

The 15.5 million additions to the existing population every year requires the opening of 66,000 new primary schools annually, raising foodgrains production from 40 lakh tonnes to 50 lakh tonnes per annum, creating 30 lakh new non-agriculture jobs every year, and accommodating 50 lakh additional labourers in the already crowded agro-sector. That 16 per cent of the world's population lives on two per cent of the land creates its own pressures--like the loss of 15 per cent of forest cover (an environmental hazard) between 1981 and 1991.

There is no use for a population policy that cannot be easily or effectively implemented. The Central and State Governments must together adopt a cafeteria approach to cater to various needs and segments of the population. It must be left to the health worker and the primary health centre to follow up on couples. Delaying the first child, spacing the second and stopping the third must remain the objective.

9

The Women's Movement in India: Action and Reflection

The women's movement in India is a rich and vibrant movement which has taken different forms in different parts of the country. Urvashi Butalia contends that the absence of a single cohesive movement, rather than being a source of weakness, may be one of the strengths of the movement. Although scattered and fragmented, it is a strong and plural movement.

One of the most enduring cliches about India is that is a country of contradictions. Like all cliches, this one too has a grain of truth in it. At the heart of the contradiction stand Indian women: for it is true to say that they are among the most oppressed in the world, and it is equally true to say that they are among the most liberated, the most articulate and perhaps even the most free. Can these two realities be simultaneously true?

During the 18 years that India had a woman as Prime Minister the country also saw increasing incidents of violence and discrimination against women. This is no different from any other time: a casual visitor to any Indian city – for example Mumbai – will see hundreds of women, young and old, working in all kinds of professions: doctors, nurses, teachers, engineers, scientists... and yet newspapers in India are full of stories of violent incidents against women, of rape, sexual harassment, sometimes even murder. But to have a woman in the highest office of the State and to simultaneously have extreme violence against women are merely the two ends of the scale. As always, a more complex reality lies in between.

Fifty years ago when India became independent, it was widely acknowledged that the battle for freedom had been fought as much by women as by men. One of the methods M K Gandhi chose to undermine the authority of the British was for Indians to defy the law which made it illegal for them to make salt. At the time, salt-making was a monopoly and earned considerable revenues for the British. Gandhi began his campaign by going on a march – the salt march – through many villages, leading finally to the sea, where he and others broke the law by making salt. No woman had been included by Gandhi in his chosen number of marchers. But nationalist women protested, and they forced him to allow them to participate.

SAROJINI NAIDU

The first to join was Sarojini Naidu, who went on to become the first woman President of the Indian National Congress in 1925. Her presence was a signal for hundreds of other women to join, and eventually the salt protest was made successful by the many women who not only made salt, but also sat openly in marketplaces selling, and indeed, buying it.

Sarojini Naidu's spirit lives on in thousands of Indian women today. Some years ago, Rojamma, a poor woman from the southern state of Andhra Pradesh, attended a literacy class. Here, she read a story which described a life very like her own. It talked about a poor woman, struggling to make ends meet, who was regularly beaten by her husband. Whatever he earned, he spent on liquor, and then, drunk and violent, he attacked her because she had no food to give him. Unable to stand the continuing violence, the woman went from house to house, to find every other woman who had the same story to tell.

They got together, and decided they would pitch their attack where it hurt most: they would picket liquor shops and stop liquor being sold. Their husbands then would have no liquor to drink, and the money they earned would be saved. Inspired by the story, Rojamma collected her friends together, and they began to picket liquor shops. The campaign spread like wildfire. In village after village, women got together, they talked, they went on strike, they beat up liquor shop owners, they refused to allow their husbands to squander money on liquor. And, they succeeded. The sale of liquor was banned in Andhra Pradesh, reluctantly, by the government for liquor brings in huge amounts of money. As a result, savings went up, violence levels dropped, and the lives of poor women began to improve.

The hundreds of thousands of Rojammas and Sarojini Naidus who are to be found all over India form part of one of the most dynamic and vibrant of political movements in India today, the women's movement.

The trajectory of this movement is usually traced from the social reform movements of the 19th century when campaigns for the betterment of the conditions of women's lives were taken up, initially by men. By the end of the century women had begun to organise themselves and gradually they took up a number of causes such as education, the conditions of women's work and so on. It was in the early part of the 20th century that women's organisations were set up, and many of the women who were active in these later became involved in the freedom movement.

Independence brought many promises and dreams for women in India – the dream of an egalitarian, just, democratic society in which both men and women would have a voice. The reality, when it began to sink in was, however, somewhat different. For all that had happened was that, despite some improvements in the status of women, patriarchy had simply taken on new and different forms.

UNFULFILLED PROMISES

By the 1960s it was clear that many of the promises of Independence were still unfulfilled. It was thus that the 1960s and 1970s saw a spate of movements in which women took part: campaigns against rising prices, movements for land rights, peasant movements. Women from different parts of the country came together to form groups both inside and outside political parties. Everywhere, in the different movements that were sweeping the country, women participated in large numbers. Everywhere, their participation resulted in transforming the movements from within.

Worried at this increase in political activity, Indira Gandhi's government declared a State of Emergency in 1975, putting a stop to all democratic political activity. Activists, both young and old, women and men, were forced to go underground or to stop all political work. It was only when the Emergency was lifted, some 18 months later, that overground political activity resumed. It was around this time that many of the contemporary women's groups began to get formed, with their members often being women with a history of involvement in other political movements.

One of the first issues to receive countrywide attention from women's groups was violence against women, specifically in the form of rape, and what came to be known in India as 'dowry deaths' – the killing of young married women for the 'dowry' or money/goods they brought with them at marriage. This was also the beginning of a process of learning for women: most protests were directed at the State. Because women were able to mobilise support, the State responded, seemingly positively, by changing the law on rape and dowry, making both more stringent.

This seemed, at the time, like a great victory. It was only later that the knowledge began to sink in that mere changes in the law meant little, unless there was a will and a machinery to implement these. And that the root of the problem of discrimination against women lay not only in the law, or with the State, but was much more widespread.

In the early campaigns, groups learnt from day to day that targeting the State was not enough and that victims also needed support. So a further level of work was needed: awareness raising or conscientisation so that violence against women could be prevented, rather than only dealt with after it had happened. Legal aid and counselling centres were set up, and attempts were made to establish women's shelters. It was only when groups began to feel sucked into the overwhelming volume of the day-to-day work of such centres that they began to feel that it was not enough to do what they now saw as 'reformist' and 'non-campaign' work. Knowledge was recognised as an important need. India is such a vast country; what did activists in Karnataka, a state in southern India, know of what was going on in Garhwal in north India? And yet, everywhere you looked, there was women's activity, activity that could not necessarily be defined as 'feminist', but that was, nonetheless, geared towards improving the conditions of women's lives.

In recent years, the euphoria of the 1970s and early 1980s, symbolised by street-level protests, campaigns in which groups mobilised at a national level, the sense of a commonality of experience cutting across class, caste, region and religion – all this seems to have gone, replaced by a more considered and complex response to issues. In many parts of India, women are no longer to be seen out on the streets protesting about this or that form of injustice. This apparent lack of a visible movement has led to the accusation that the women's movement is dead or dying.

Other whipping sticks have been brought out: little has happened to improve women's lives, so how can the movement be called successful? Activists within the movement are urban, Western, and middle class, so the movement was considered an alien thing, a Western product. It has little to do with the lives of thousands of poor, rural, underprivileged women all over India.

These allegations make the classic mistake: they judge a complex reality by that part of it that is most visible. Because urban, middle-class women are visible and articulate, therefore they must be the only participants in the women's movement.

BACKBONE

The reality is somewhat different. While the participation of urban, middle class women is undeniable, it is not they who make up the backbone of the movement, or of the many, different campaigns that are generally seen as comprising the movement. The anti-alcohol agitation in Andhra Pradesh, and similar campaigns in other parts of India were started and sustained by poor, low-caste, often working-class women. The movement to protect the environment was begun by poor women in a village called Reni in the northern hill regions of India, and only after that did it spread to other parts of the country. There are any number of such examples.

One of the biggest challenges women have had to face in recent years is the growing influence of the religious right in India. Right-wing groups have built much of their support on the involvement of women: offering to help them with domestic problems, enabling them to enter the public space in a limited way, and all the while ensuring that the overall ideology within which they operate remains firmly patriarchal. For activists too, this has posed major problems. It has forced them to confront the fact that they cannot assume a solidarity as women that cuts across class, religion, caste, ethnic difference. And yet, they must hold fast to such an assumption if they are to work with women: for how, as an activist, do you deal with a woman who takes part in a violent right wing demonstration one day, and comes to you for help as a victim of domestic violence the next?

erhaps the most significant development for women in the last few decades has been the introduction of 33% reservation for women in local, village-level elections. In the early days, when this move was introduced, there was considerable scepticism. How will women cope? Are they equipped to be leaders? Will this mean any real change, or will it merely mean that the men will take a backseat and use the women as a front to implement what they want? While all these problems still remain, in a greater or lesser degree, what is also true is that more and more women have shown that once they have power, they are able to use it, to the benefit of society in general and women in particular.

The women's movement in India today is a rich and vibrant movement, which has spread to various parts of the country. It is often said that there is no one single cohesive movement in the country, but a number of fragmented campaigns. Activists see this as one of the strengths of the movement which takes different forms in different parts. While the movement may be scattered all over India, they feel it is nonetheless a strong and plural force.

It is important to recognise that for a country of India's magnitude, change in male-female relations and the kinds of issues the women's movement is focusing on, will not come easy. For every step the movement takes forward, there will be a possible backlash, a possible regression. And it is this that makes for the contradictions, this that makes it possible for there to be women who can aspire to, and attain, the highest political office in the country, and for women to continue to have to confront patriarchy within the home, in the workplace, throughout their lives. As activists never tire of repeating: out of the deepest repression is born the greatest resistance.

10

Status of Muslim Women in India

INTRODUCTION

Although caste disadvantage has been well documented as an important and pervasive axis of social inequality to India, disadvantage and discrimination do not end with the Scheduled Castes and Tribes. Religious minorities are also disadvantaged, but this fact is less well documented and recognised; and though Muslims are a heterogeneous minority, they have had a historically 'other' status which has made them vulnerable to discrimination, for example, in access to health and education. Thus, frequently, the identities of class, gender, and religious community overlap to create discrimination and inequality in most spheres of life in India.

In modern day India, the socio-economic status of women in Muslim communities, along with their political participation ratio and the need for legal reform, are causes for concern and need attention. This point cannot be overstated in a context where, in 1983, the Gopal Singh Committee instituted by the government, declared Muslims as a 'backward' community in India.1 A central feature of this 'backwardness' is the appalling educational and socio-economic status of Muslims in India, particularly Muslim women.

According to the 1991 Government of India Census, there are over 48 million Muslim women in India.2 Currently available fragmented statistical and micro studies e.g. on Muslim women reiterate that the majority are among the most disadvantaged, economically impoverished, and politically marginalised sections of the Indian society. These studies suggest that, like other women, Muslim women too are not homogeneous, and are differentiated along the fault-lines of class, caste, community, and region. Their lives are similarly located at the intersection of gender, family, and community within the dynamic context of Indian society, polity, and economy. At the conceptual level, this paper seeks to investigate the status of Muslim women within a theoretical framework of social inequality and inter-group disparity.

On the completion of more than five decades of independence, women in Muslim communities face considerable challenges as citizens of India and as members of India's largest minority. Their poor socio-economic status reflects a lack of social opportunity which, though not a feature exclusive to Muslim women, is exacerbated by their marginal status within an overall context of social disadvantage for most Indian women. This point was highlighted in a study of 39 districts in 1981 (where the population of Muslims ranged from 20 percent to 95 percent-which could be considered a fairly representative sample of the status of Muslims in India).

In the study, the literacy rate of Muslim women was found to be 21.91 percent-lower than even the poor national average of 24.82 percent. According to government reports, Muslim women are among the poorest, educationally disenfranchised, economically vulnerable, politically marginalized group in the country.

Most Muslim women remain 'invisible' workers in the informal economy. The Muslim share in public employment is less than 3 percent. Within this picture of marginalisation, it is a predictable certainty that the corresponding figures for Muslim women are further skewed towards the bottom. A lack of information on Muslim women contributes to the reinforcement of cultural stereotypes, serving to obfuscate their life experiences and struggles. Consequently, the notion that Muslim women's status in India is attributable to certain intrinsic, immutable 'Islamic' features or that their social status derives solely from Muslim laws, is widely prevalent.

This study highlights the distorted status of Muslim women in India both in the context of gender and minority rights. There are generally two reasons for their weak social status; one, their status as women in a patriarchal society is already somewhat lower to the male members and the weak legal and social infrastructure rendering them vulnerable to the social injustices, two, the socially and economically impoverished condition of the Muslim community disallows the development of norms that would discourage gender bias and render the women free and respectable members of the society.

GENERAL STATUS OF MUSLIMS IN INDIA

Some 101.59 million Muslims inhabit India.5 With the exception of Indonesia and Pakistan, it is one of the largest population of Muslims in a single country in the world. Muslim communities in India are geographically scattered, culturally diverse and economically disparate. A majority of Muslims in India live in Uttar Pradesh, Bihar and West Bengal. The following table presents comparison of the Muslims and Hindus in different areas of India:

States (where Muslim Population exceeds 5%)	Muslim Proportion 2001/(1961)	%age of population under 6 yrs Muslim/(Hindu) (Indicator of current/ future growth)	Literacy, 2001 Muslim/ (Hindu)
Jammu & Kashmir	67%	15.4% (13.3)	47.3% (71.2)
Assam	31%	22% (14.5)	48.4% (70)
West Bengal	25.2%	18.7% (12.7)	57.5% (72.4)
Kerala	24.7%	15% (10.8)	89.4% (90.2)
UP	18.5%	20.9% (18.6)	47.8% (58)
Bihar	16.5%	22% (19.9)	42% (47.9)
Jharkhand	13.8%	21.1% (17.9)	55.6% (54.6)
India	13.4% (10.7%)	18.7% (15.6)	59.1% (65.1)
Karnataka	12.2%	16.1% (13.3)	70.1% (65.6)
Uttaranchal	11.9%	21.2% (15.4)	51.1% (74.1)
Delhi	11.7%	18.5% (14.3)	66.6% (82.8)

Contd...

States (where Muslim Population exceeds 5%)	Muslim Proportion 2001/(1961)	%age of population under 6 yrs Muslim/(Hindu) (Indicator of current/ future growth)	Literacy, 2001 Muslim/ (Hindu)
Maharashtra	10.6%	16.2% (14)	78.1% (76.2)
Andhra Pardesh	9.2%	14.9% (13.2)	68% (59.4)
Gujrat	9.1%	15.7% (14.9)	73.5% (68.3)
Rajasthan	8.5%	21% (18.8)	56.6% (60.2)
Tripura	8%	18.6% (13)	60.9% (75.3)
Goa	6.8%	15.2% (10.9)	75.4% (81.9)
Madhya Pradesh	6.4%	17.9% (18)	70.3% (62.8)
Haryana	5.8%	24.5% (15.4)	40% (69.4)
Tamil Nadu	5.6%	12.9% (11.5)	82.9% (72)

At a glance, Muslims have a poor socio-economic status, with a marginal presence in public life. More than 50 percent of India's 101.59 million Muslims live below the poverty line, with a monthly income of Rs 150 or less. Hindus who constitute 82.2 percent of the population form 85.3 percent of the elite; Christians comprising 2.6 percent of the population are 3.5 percent of the elite; Jains constituting 0.5 percent of the population are 2.8 percent of the elite; while Muslims who are 11.2 percent of the population constitute only 4.5 percent of the elite-with women faring the worst.

In addition, Muslim representation in Parliament and State Assemblies is declining. There were 46 Muslims in the Lok Sabha (lower house of Parliament) in 1982, a figure which went down to 26 in the 1991 elections. These problems have been a subject of debate within the Muslim community. In its first meeting in January 1992, the Muslim Intelligentsia Forum demanded the attention of the government, political parties, the media and the ulema to the situation of Muslims in India. The Muslim Intelligentsia Forum held subsequent meetings in various towns and cities in India. In September 1997, for the first time, a group of past and present Muslim MPs met to address the educational and economic disadvantage of the community.

Muslims' share in public employment in All-India and Central Services is less than 3 percent. Within this picture of poor overall employment statistics, it is a predictable certainty that the corresponding figures for Muslim women are lower still.

MUSLIM WOMEN IN INDIA THROUGH THE AGES

The position of women in any society is the index to the standard of social organisation. In Indian society, the status of women has changed from time to time. Though women in India do not constitute an undifferentiated, homogenous category, yet, little information exists on Indian Muslim women.

However, the perception that Muslim women's social status in India can be ascribed to a certain intrinsic, immutable feature of Islam or that their legal status derives solely from reference to Muslim laws is widely prevalent.

As a result of this misconception, Muslim women are often considered as 'separate' or 'different' from Indian society, reinforcing cultural stereotypes and obscuring their contemporary realities. Mainstream historical narrative with its emphasis on the rise and fall of the Muslim empire excludes Muslim women.

Although Muslim women were generally absent from public life during this period, several women from royalty were authors and poets-or even a Sultan as in the case of Raziya Sultana (1236-1240) in India.

At the turn of the twentieth century the topic of female education was taken up by Muslim communities. Several Muslim women made pioneering contributions to female education. Figures for Muslim girls' participation in educational institutions during the early decades of the twentieth century surpassed figures for the national average. Muslim women also participated in campaigns against female seclusion and legal discrimination, and played an active part in the emerging women's movement. This trend suffered a setback due to the social, political and economic upheavals in, during and after the partition of India in 1947. In the wake of the trauma and large-scale migrations during 1947, and a subsequent lack of political presence, it was extremely difficult for Muslim women to articulate their concerns, both within the community and as citizens of India.

MUSLIM WOMEN IN MODERN DAY INDIA

The economic differentiation constitutes probably the primary source of differentiation in status between Muslim and Hindu women in the aggregate, since the household's level of assets ownership, occupation and income possibilities critically determine the basic conditions of life of the women. However, there are significant regional differences in this: Muslims are generally poor in the north (especially rural areas) and east, but less so in the south. It is significant to understand the status of Muslims as a community in general and then evaluate the status of Muslim women in particular.

Like Scheduled Castes, Muslims are disproportionately represented among the poor and have the lowest per capita income indicators. This is ascribed not only to lack of access to asset ownership, but also to poor educational attainment and occupational patterns which show clustering in low-paid activities, as well as the concentration of the Muslim population in the economically backward regions of the country.

As with women from other communities, Muslim women are differentiated across gender, class, caste and community, and are subject to the interface between gender and community within the Indian social, political and economic context.

At the same time, Muslim women's location in modern India also derives from their status as a minority, which colours their life experience and self-perception in distinct ways, and in this respect they differ from women belonging to other communities. After five decades of independence the majority of Muslim women are among the most disadvantaged, least literate, economically impoverished and politically marginalised sections of Indian society. The social and economic issues confronting women in Muslim communities mandate attention as does the violation of their rights as citizens of India.

Educational Portfolio in India Literacy and Gender Gap

	Jain	Christians	Buddhists	Sikh	Hindu	India Average	Muslim
Literacy	94.1%	80.3%	72.7%	69.4%	65.1%	65%	59.1%
Gender	7%	10%	25%	15%	28.3%	28%	26%

Source: http://members.tripod.com/~INDIA_RESOURCE/religion-demographics.html

Gender gap has been calculated as the difference between male and female literacy divided by male literacy. In other words, it represents the proportion of women who should have been educated for the literacy rates in the community to have been absolutely even.

ISSUES CONFRONTING MUSLIM WOMEN IN INDIA

In a study of 39 districts, where the population of Muslims ranged from 20 percent to 95 percent (which could be considered a fairly representative sample of the Muslims in India)-the literacy rate of Muslim women was found to be 21.91 percent, which was lower than the average of 24.82 percent for the whole country.

Within this broader picture of social disadvantage, the literacy levels of Muslim men and women are further skewed towards the bottom. Figures for female literacy are almost identical for both Hindu (75 percent) and Muslim (76.1 percent) women in rural India.

Almost 59.5 percent of Muslim women are illiterate in urban India, as compared to 42.2 percent of Hindu women and 22.7 percent of Christian women who come under this category. There is some semblance of parity between urban Hindu (17.2 percent) and Muslim (18.5 percent) women with reference to primary education which widens considerably for corresponding figures for middle school-25.3 percent for urban Hindu women, and 16.8 percent for Muslim women-the difference being much greater when compared to Christian women (33.4 percent). Only 4.3 percent of urban Muslim women have secondary education, compared to 10.7 percent of Hindu women and 20.8 percent of Christian women.

The number of urban Muslim female graduates is negligible (0.8 percent, against 4.2 percent of Hindu women and 5.5 percent of Christian women).13

TABLE 1: Women's Education Level by Community

Community	1	2	3	4	5	6
SC	68.79	0.93	6.47	12.36	7.19	4.25
ST	71.73	0.00	9.45	8.46	8.99	1.37
OBC	56.63	0.93	6.71	17.96	12.34	5.43
Others	36.32	0.56	7.42	27.15	16.87	11.68
Muslim	57.66	1.80	10.51	16.75	9.71	3.56
Total	57.55	1.80	7.43	17.27	11.08	5.74

Source: Zoya Hasan, Ritu Menon, Unequal Citizens, New Delhi, Oxford University Press, 2004, p. 48.

TABLE 2: Regional Distribution of Women's Education Level: Rural North

Community	1	2	3	4	5	6
SC	88.06	1.00	1.99	4.98	1.99	1.99
ST	88.89	0.00	0.00	11.11	0.00	0.00
OBC	82.72	0.00	1.57	10.47	2.09	3.14
Others	58.62	0.00	3.45	17.24	10.34	10.34
Muslim	83.58	3.02	2.35	4.58	4.25	2.23
Total	82.29	0.71	2.00	8.46	3.18	3.35

Source: Zoya Hasan, Ritu Menon, Unequal Citizens, New Delhi, Oxford University Press, 2004, p. 49.

TABLE 3: Regional Distribution of Women's Education Level: Urban North

Community	1	2	3	4	5	6
SC	65.57	1.64	4.10	12.30	9.02	7.38
ST	85.71	0.00	0.00	14.29	0.00	0.00
OBC	51.14	0.76	4.92	18.18	11.36	13.64
Others	25.26	1.05	3.16	12.11	21.58	36.84
Muslim	74.36	2.74	2.57	4.56	6.97	8.80
Total	49.37	1.22	3.94	13.74	13.25	18.47

Source: Zoya Hasan, Ritu Menon, Unequal Citizens, New Delhi, Oxford University Press, 2004, p.49.

TABLE 4: Regional Distribution of Women's Education Level: Rural South

Community	1	2	3	4	5	6
SC	46.88	3.12	12.50	18.75	12.50	6.25
ST						
OBC	24.66	1.37	16.44	30.14	23.29	4.11
Others	20.00	0.00	5.00	40.00	25.00	10.00
Muslim	23.64	0.75	14.01	39.23	18.21	4.20
Total	29.07	1.52	13.64	29.73	20.57	5.48

Source: Zoya Hasan, Ritu Menon, Unequal Citizens, New Delhi, Oxford University Press, 2004, p. 49.

TABLE 5: Regional Distribution of Women's Education Level: Urban South

Community	1	2	3	4	5	6
SC	17.74	1.61	8.06	22.58	33.87	16.13
ST	14.29	0.00	14.29	28.57	42.86	0.00
OBC	19.42	0.00	9.35	29.5	31.65	10.07
Others	15.62	0.00	3.12	28.12	34.38	18.75
Muslim	22.14	1.04	11.02	35.85	20.83	9.11
Total	19.09	0.54	8.87	29.16	30.51	11.83

Source: Zoya Hasan, Ritu Menon, Unequal Citizens, New Delhi, Oxford University Press, 2004, p.50.

TABLE 6: Regional Distribution of Women's Education Level: Urban East

Community	1	2	3	4	5	6
SC	34.38	0.00	20.31	21.88	17.19	6.25
ST	33.33	0.00	33.33	33.33	0.00	0.00
OBC	20.00	2.50	12.50	32.50	17.50	15.00
Others	23.76	0.00	8.91	25.74	28.71	12.87
Muslim	41.72	1.45	16.26	25.46	10.84	4.26

Source: Zoya Hasan, Ritu Menon, Unequal Citizens, New Delhi, Oxford University Press, 2004, p.50.

TABLE 7: Regional Distribution of Women's Education Level: Rural West

Community	1	2	3	4	5	6
SC	63.64	0.00	0.00	13.64	18.18	4.55
ST	87.50	0.00	0.00	12.50	0.00	0.00
OBC	56.25	3.12	9.38	15.62	12.50	3.12
Others	37.50	0.00	0.00	43.75	12.50	6.25
Muslim	56.66	1.45	14.29	20.10	5.08	2.42
Total	60.27	1.18	4.05	19.78	11.29	3.43

Source: Zoya Hasan, Ritu Menon, Unequal Citizens, New Delhi, Oxford University Press, 2004, p.50.

TABLE 8: Regional Distribution of Women's Education Level: Urban West

Community	1	2	3	4	5	6
SC	40.91	0.00	0.09	25.00	0.09	15.91
ST	42.86	0.00	14.29	0.00	42.86	0.00
OBC	36.76	2.94	8.82	22.06	16.18	13.24
Others	23.94	0.00	9.86	25.35	26.76	14.08
Muslim	34.88	1.79	8.75	28.77	18.65	7.17
Total	33.48	1.19	9.34	24.22	19.32	12.45

Source: Zoya Hasan, Ritu Menon, Unequal Citizens, New Delhi, Oxford University Press, 2004, p.50.

Unlike the percentage difference between Muslim, Hindu and Christian women in primary education, Muslim women in both rural and urban India lag behind their counterparts in school enrollment from the very beginning. This initial disadvantage is further exacerbated across subsequent educational enrollment categories.

The figure of 32.8 percent for rural Muslim females attending school in the 5-9 age group (compared to 40.6 percent Hindu women) or 1.4 percent for Muslim rural female enrolment for the 20+ age group (7.4 percent for Hindu women) is still more favourable than the corresponding figures for urban India. The enrolment figure of 52.1 percent for urban Muslim females compares poorly to the corresponding figure of 70.7 percent for Hindu females, which further widens across subsequent age categories to end with 4.7 percent of Muslim females attending educational institutions, compared to 10.2 percent of Hindu women or 18.2 percent of Christian women.

Clearly, Muslim women in urban India are much worse off than their rural counterparts, not only in terms of their overall educational status as citizens of India, but also in terms of their relatively poor educational status when compared to Hindu or Christian women. This trend is all the more alarming when this situation is compared to the advances in Muslim female education achieved at the turn of the century. This educational disadvantage of women in Muslim communities require immediate attention.

The Indian government has failed to secure primary and secondary education for most of its citizens and its policies have deprived people of their right to education. It could also be assumed that Muslim girls' schooling is not always encouraged. The female literacy rate is an appalling 28.1 percent. An improvement in the overall literacy rates for Muslims would not just lead to a corresponding increase in Muslim enrollment in universities and professional courses, but also ensure more social opportunity for Muslim women (and men). This initial disadvantage, i.e. Muslim women's poor literacy rates, completely precludes the possibility of their entering institutions of higher education. Due to this reason the Aligarh Muslim University and the Jamia Millia Islamia-minority institutions with the specific aim of furthering education among Muslims (both male and female) in India are unable to have a majority of Muslim students in their professional schools.

The lack of social opportunities for Muslim women is a crucial issue needing urgent action. An improvement in literacy rates would directly influence Muslim women's socio-economic and political status as citizens of India.

EMPLOYMENT AND MUSLIM WOMEN

Lack of active participation in the work force is a potent reason for the dismal socio-economic status of Muslim women as they have the lowest work participation rate (WPR), with a large gap between the WPRs for Muslim women and Hindu or Christian women.

Sixty percent of Muslim women are self-employed which is the highest percentage among all three religious categories. Figures for Muslim women's employment as regular workers in urban areas (15.7 percent as compared to 27.7 percent for Hindu women and 51.5 percent for Christian women) highlight their marginal presence in salaried jobs. Figures for rural areas however, dismal as they are, also indicate a more or less similar employment status for Hindu (3.6 percent) and Muslim (3.0 percent) women.16

The high self-employment rates and the corresponding low participation of Muslim women as salaried workers indicate their marginal presence as workers in the formal economy. This does not imply the absence of Muslim women as workers; rather it indicates their 'invisibility' as informal workers. In the absence of existing research and analysis in the area of Muslim women's employment, it is difficult to pinpoint specific causes behind their poor employment status. Although, their educational status must presumably exert a significant influence on the form and levels of Muslim women's employment in both urban and rural areas. Self-empowerment is crucial for the members of Muslim communities-especially Muslim women to debate among themselves reasons and solutions for their poor educational and employment status, their precarious economic situation, as well as the need for legal reform and greater political participation, and the possibilities of overcoming patriarchal structures within their own communities.

INDIAN LAWS: SUBJUGATING MUSLIM WOMEN?

Though aimed at eradication of social evils, the various social legislation in India passed from time to time are mainly responsible for the deteriorating condition of Muslim women. These legislations brought upward trend in the status of women in India, but it is only for non-Muslim Indian women. Personal law (i.e. laws covering family relations, marriage, divorce, inheritance, custody rights, etc.) is a contested arena for the women's movement as well as for Hindu and Muslim conservatives.

It not only defines the relationship between men and women in marriage and family relations but also marks the relationship between women and the state. While civil and criminal laws in post-independent India are secular, the respective religious laws govern personal laws. Accordingly, Muslim women came under the purview of Muslim personal (family) law.

The passage of the Hindu Code Bill Shah Bano controversy, and Imrana case brought Muslim personal law, which had not been subject to any legislative changes since the 1937 Shariat Act and the 1939 Dissolution of Muslim Marriages Act, back into focus.

Legislation on women in post-independence India faced stiff opposition from Hindu and Muslim conservatives. The Assembly debates preceding the passage of the Hindu Code Bill-which gave Hindu women the right to divorce and allowed for inter-caste marriage and monogamy-symbolised the cross-communal patriarchal collusion in opposing any pro-women legislation. The Special Marriages Act, 1952, which allowed two Indians to marry without renouncing their religion provoked strong opposition from Hindu and Muslim Members of parliament (MPs).

The debates also highlighted the transformation of a women's rights debate into a discourse where personal codes merged with perceptions of communal 'identity'. At another level, the debate also translated into a set of competing concessions between Hindu and Muslim men. As Dr. Mookerjee and Pundit Govind Malviya asserted, 'Hindus would accept monogamy only when Muslims did, that divorce could not take place in "Ram Rajya" and that they were against a daughter's share in her father's property since that would be imitating Muslims.'

In 1973, in an amendment relating to the rights of divorced women to maintenance under the Criminal Procedure Code, the word 'wife' in Section 125 was amended to include a 'divorced wife'. This provoked protests from the Muslim League whose members argued that the amendment violated Muslim personal law.

The amendment went on to exclude Muslim women from the provisions of Section 125 if they had already received payment due to them under Muslim law. However, in a subsequent judgment (Bai Tahira vs Ali Hussain) the Supreme Court held that, 'the payment of illusory amounts by way of customary or Personal Law requirement will be considered in the reduction of maintenance rate but cannot annihilate the rate unless it is a reasonable substitute'.

The provision of triple talaq (unilateral divorce by saying the word talaq three times in one sitting) is another area within Muslim law where women face discrimination.19 The threat of verbal divorce (invested with men) acts as a perpetual legal and psychological threat against Muslim women.

This was acknowledged by National Commission of Women (NCW) member Syeda Hameed at a seminar on Muslim women in Bombay, when she called for personal laws to be amended 'so as to help ease the sufferings of Muslim women'.20 In 1986,21 Shah Bano, a 73-year-old Muslim woman was thrown out of her house by her husband after 43 years of marriage after he used the triple talaq. In 1977 Shah Bano's husband stopped the payment of Rs. 200 as maintenance, upon which she filed an application for maintenance of Rs. 500 under Section 125 of the Criminal Procedure Code.

Her husband subsequently divorced her, paying Rs. 3,000 as final settlement. A judicial magistrate, however, ordered him to pay a sum of Rs 25 (approximately US $0.50), which was later raised to Rs. 179.20 by the Madhya Pradesh High Court. Shah Bano's former husband appealed to the Supreme Court of India and argued that Muslim personal law did not oblige ex-husbands to provide maintenance for their former wives.

The Supreme Court dismissed his appeal and upheld the maintenance order under Section 125 of the Criminal Procedure Code. Subsequently, Parliament passed the Muslim Women Protection of Rights on Divorce Bill-which denied Muslim women the right to maintenance under constitutional law. The judgment and subsequent Muslim Women's Bill generated much debate and led to wide scale mobilisation by women's groups on the issue of personal law. It also highlighted the disjunction between constitutional law premised on the principle of sexual equality and religious laws, which discriminate on the basis of this very category.

Parties like the Jamaat-e-Islami have argued that Muslim personal law is divine, beyond human intervention and that any attempt to change it would represent an erosion of Muslim cultural identity. Reactions from the Muslim Personal Law Board were equally intolerant, which declared its intention to set up 'Islamic courts' in order to dispense justice according to the Quran. The BJP appropriated the women's rights debate by aggressively campaigning for a Uniform Civil Code, which would replace Muslim personal law. Equating nationalism with the adoption of a Uniform Civil Code, the Hindu right-wing portrayed Muslim reluctance towards reform in personal law as 'minority appeasement' and an impediment to national progress. The fact that many Muslims wanted reform within personal law without being considered culturally inferior or unpatriotic was completely overlooked.

Since independence, successive Indian governments have avoided taking any legislative measures to end discrimination in personal laws. Such a policy contradicts India's commitment to the Convention on the Elimination of All Forms of Discrimination Against Women (CEDAW) which upholds the principle of equality among men and women in the family.

The status of Indian Muslim women mandates attention not only because it is a marker of women's progress, but also because it is difficult to institute legal reforms without simultaneous progress in Muslim women's educational status and economic autonomy.

The latest Imrana case signifies a weakness in the implementation of the Islamic system in the Indian society. Imrana, a 28-year-old woman, a mother of 5 was allegedly raped by her father-in-law, in Muzaffarnagar in June 2005. The village panchayat ruled that according to the Sharia laws, "zina" had been committed, and the rapist was a blood relative of her husband, therefore her marriage was anulled.

Instead, she was told to marry the rapist, i.e the father-in-law, and start thinking of her present husband as her son. The matter was then referred to the Islamic scholars of the Darul-Uloom in Deoband, who issued a fatwa upholding the judgement of the panchayat, saying it was in accordance with the Sharia.

The fatwa has been challenged and condemned by many human rights and women rights organisations. Apparently, there is no legal protection for women who are victims of such crimes. The All India Muslim Personal Law Board has also refused to overturn the local fatwa.

A member of All India Muslim Personal Law Board (AIMPLB) Hazrat Mufti Fazil-ur-Rehman charged that the alleged rape of Imrana and the fatwa issued by Deoband was being given hype in order to "defame" Islam. He asserted that though the rape had not been proved yet but Imrana must separate from her husband for the whole life and her husband should pay for her expenses.

The appropriation of Muslim women's issues by a vocal and politically influential male Muslim constituency for political purposes poses a considerable challenge to Muslim women's legal empowerment.

This was highlighted during the Shah Bano case and the passage of the Muslim Women's Bill in 1986. In a context where the Shari'a is used to justify women's subordination, it is imperative for Muslim women in India to enter the discourse on the Shari'a with reference to personal law, and challenge their historic marginalisation from religious knowledge. Furthermore, it is crucial for Muslims-women and men-to debate among themselves the possible reasons and remedies for their poor status as citizens of India.

The political ascendance of the Hindu right wing and its inherent link between politics and religion has threatened India's secular fabric. The rise of communal violence in the last two decades has undermined secular law and violated constitutional ideals of religious non-discrimination, protection of human rights, implementation of social justice and the equality of all Indian citizens-as well as principles of international human rights law. Right-wing illiberalism, communal prejudice and intolerance of diversity bodes ill for all Indian women; in the case of Muslim women it heightens physical and economic insecurity, limits possibilities of renegotiating their status with Muslim men and precipitates Muslim militancy.

CONCLUSION

The Muslim women are among the poorest, educationally disenfranchised, economically vulnerable, politically marginalised group in India. Their poor socio-economic status reflects a lack of social opportunity, which, though not a feature exclusive to Muslim women, is exacerbated by their marginal status within an overall context of social disadvantage for most Indian women.24

The impoverished status of a large number of Muslim women in India underlines the urgency for further inquiry in this area and also the need for active intervention by state agencies to implement policies to redress this imbalance and ensure Muslim women's full and equal participation as Indian citizens.

The civil society in India is vibrant and has taken initiatives to improve the situation. There were regional initiatives like the formation of the Minorities Vikas Manch (Forum) in Jaipur, Rajasthan, to raise Muslim women's literacy levels in the state and to create awareness among the state's Muslims about state welfare schemes. A series of 'Public Hearings of Muslim Women', instituted by the National Commission for Women, highlighted the economic problems facing Muslim women. 'The overriding concern of these women was the lack of educational facilities for their children. The other concerns were lack of health facilities, lack of hygiene, no housing, no vocational opportunities.' Furthermore, a group of Muslim women, lawyers and Muslim Personal Law Board members in Bombay worked on a model nikahnama (marriage contract) stipulating a set of minimal conditions to safeguard women's rights in the marriage contract.

They hope to discuss the nikahnama with the Muslim Personal Law Board. At a seminar on Muslim women in Bombay held in collaboration with the National Commission for Women, a resolution calling for a dialogue with the Muslim Personal Law Board, and favouring reforms in Muslim personal law, was passed.25 As Muslim personal law in post-independent India is yet to undergo any reform, with a politically influential section of the Muslim community resisting change, this is an important development. It symbolizes Muslim women and men's determination to challenge existing laws and renegotiate ideas on women's rights which, in turn, are inextricably linked to current debates on Muslim women and Islam.

It is crucial for members of Muslim communities, Muslim women and men, to introspect and debate among themselves as to the reasons and remedies for their economic vulnerability and poor educational and employment status, and to consider possible remedies. There is also a need for debate and mobilisation by Muslim women on legal reform in order to overcome patriarchal structures with Muslim communities. The debate on legal reform is linked to debates on women and Islam. Muslim women in India need to participate in the contemporary debate on Islam and women's rights. It is imperative for Indian Muslim women to reclaim their right to religious knowledge, enter the discourse on the Shari'a and challenge their historic marginalisation from religious knowledge as well as its discriminatory inter-pretations.

The acknowledgement of the universality of women's rights by the international community is relevant to the debate on Islam and women's rights, particularly with reference to women's rights in the family. The formation of forums and associations of Muslim end and women's initiatives in the 1990s is an important step towards facilitating public debate on Muslim women's issues. Muslim women and men must collaborate with individuals and organisations that are committed to the realisation of women's human rights. The alliance of Muslim women with the women's movement in India, as well as movements for secularism, democracy and human rights, are crucial for forging a common front against forces opposed to women's self-determination.

11

Overview of Socio-economic Situation

The information presented is based on the data collected in 1997 by formulation missions to Madhya Pradesh and Bihar and other studies undertaken for the present reformulation mission, including Participatory Rural Appraisal (PRAs) studies done in both states. This has been complemented by additional information gathered by this reformulation mission from village women and men, different Government offices and non-governmental organizations (NGOs).

BACKGROUND

Rural Poverty and the Status of Women at National Level

The household consumer expenditure (HCE) survey conducted during 1993/94 showed that India had slightly less than 40% of the population, or over 325 million people, under the officially defined poverty line. Of these, over 280 million lived in rural areas. In other words, 35% of the households and about 40% of the population in rural areas live below the poverty line.

In the first two and a half decades after independence, the incidence of poverty fluctuated but showed no sustained decline. Since 1977/78, however, the proportion of poor has been declining. Available statistics show that this trend became particularly visible during 1983-1993/94, when the proportion of the poor as measured by headcount ratio (HCR) decreased by 16%, the depth of poverty as measured by the poverty gap index (PGI) by 30%, and the severity of poverty as measured by the relative squared poverty gap by 45%.

The rate of decrease in the proportion of the poor, however, is slow, at about 2% per annum in the 1980s, and poverty remains widespread. In absolute terms, the number of poor in India increased from about 164 million in 1951 to over 325 million in 1993. Of the estimated 1.3 billion poor in the world, about 27% are in India. Given that India's share of world population is only about 15%, it has a disproportionately higher share of the world's poor.

The key features of the rural poverty in India are as follows:

* Among rural households, landless agricultural labourers have the highest incidence of poverty (51%), followed by non-agricultural rural labour (35%). Of the total rural poor, almost 42% are agricultural labourers and about 33% self-employed households in agriculture. Overall, 42% of rural poor households are landless and over 80% of them cultivate less than 1 ha of land.
* Among the social groups, scheduled tribes (STs) have the highest proportion of the poor (54%), followed by scheduled castes (SCs, 50%). Of the total rural poor population, scheduled castes account for 27% and scheduled tribes about 15%, although their share in the entire population is only 18 % and 11%, respectively. In essence, caste and, to some extent, ethnicity continue to determine the ownership of land and thus poverty.
* Scheduled tribe populations in India suffer from other forms of human deprivation than the lack of material well being. While the tribal population accounts for only about 8% of the total population, it constitutes 40% of the displaced population. The literacy rate among STs is only 24%, compared to 52% in the general population in 1991. Among the rural women of the tribal population, the literacy rate is only 13%. Similarly, while gross primary-school enrolment among STs has increased over time, and the gap with the rest of the population may disappear very soon, the dropout rate remains high.

* There is a significant inter-and intra-state variation in the incidence of rural poverty in India. Among the states having the highest proportion of the poor in 1993/94, Bihar ranks first (66%), followed by Assam (57%), Orissa (57%), West Bengal (52%), Maharashtra (51%) and Arunanchal Pradesh (48%). The three eastern states of West Bengal, Bihar and Orissa account for over 42% of the rural poor.
* Disaggregated data at sub-state level show highly uneven change in the headcount ratios within the state and a very high incidence of poverty in certain regions. Overall, there is an almost contiguous region encompassing four regions of eastern Maharashtra, two southern regions of Madhya Pradesh, all of Uttar Pradesh except the western region, all of Bihar and West Bengal, and five regions of the northeastern states.

In the last quarter of a century, Indian women have significantly improved their overall well being. Yet women in India remain one of the most disadvantaged groups in society. The sex ratio has been in more or less constant decline since 1901 (when it was 944) and has dropped to 927. Only 39% of women are literate (against 64% for men) and only 34% of births are attended by trained health personnel. The maternal mortality rate is high, and India accounts for about one fourth of total maternity-related deaths in the world. The death rate for female children under five is 29 per thousand, against 25 among male children of the same age group. Of the 324 million illiterates enumerated in the 1991 census, 61% were women and girls. Some 39% of the girls drop out before completing primary education and 57% before completing upper primary. The average age at marriage has increased but is still low at 19.5 years, and some 30% of the girls are married between 15 and 19.

Over 90% of rural women workers are unskilled and about 90% of women are engaged in the informal/unorganized sector. Wage rates in agriculture are on average 30-50% less than for men. Women shoulder the entire burden of household activities and child-care responsibilities and 58% of women's work time is spent in such activities. Female casual labourers in rural India show the highest incidence of poverty of any occupational category, male or female. A disproportionate burden of poverty is suffered by female-headed households. At the same time, the delivery structures of credit, technical advice, etc., do not reach them, because institutions are slow to recognize women as heads of households.

NATIONAL TRIBAL POLICY

India has about 532 scheduled tribes (STs) speaking over 100 different languages, with each tribe having its own ethnic and cultural identity. According to the 1991 census, the population of STs in the country was 67.8 million constituting around 8% of the total population. Over half the tribal population is concentrated in five states-Madhya Pradesh (15.4 million), Bihar (6.6 million), Orissa (7.0 million), Andhra Pradesh (4.2 million) and West Bengal (3.8 million). Madhya Pradesh accounts for 23% and Bihar 9.7% of the total tribal population in the country.

Historically, tribal communities were characterized by a lifestyle distinct from agrarian communities. They subsisted on different combinations of shifting cultivation, hunting and gathering of forest products: all activities closely linked with forests. Their cultures celebrated and fostered this close bond with nature while also emphasizing communal ownership and consumption, closely-knit kinship structures, and minimal hierarchies.

The British colonial rule either appropriated their forests or drastically curtailed their access to them while suppressing shifting cultivation. It also imposed a system of revenue collection, which, while re-constructing natural communities into administrative 'revenue villages', also opened the doors for exploitative non-tribal moneylenders and traders to start settling in tribal areas. Tribal rebellions, both against State interventions curtailing their access to local natural resources and exploitation by outsiders, resulted in special laws being framed for many tribal areas in recognition of the unique self-regulatory cultural traits of tribal communities.

The Scheduled District Act promulgated in 1874 delineated tribal areas as 'scheduled areas'. The Government of India Act of 1935 further classified these areas into two categories, i.e. the northeastern tribal region and other backward tribal regions. The former was totally excluded from the ambit of major Indian laws, whereas the latter were partially excluded. After Independence, the tribals were accorded special rights and protection under Article 342 of the Constitution with the Government of India's tribal development policy aiming to bring them the benefits of economic development without eroding their traditional culture and identity. Independent India has continued with the 'scheduling' of tribal areas and tribes introduced by the British.

Tribal areas outside the northeastern region, including the study area, come under the Fifth Schedule of the Constitution. The State Governor, or a Tribal Advisory Council Chair, can make special provisions for the administration of Schedule Five areas besides waiving or amending any existing law considered detrimental to tribal interests or in conflict with their traditional values and culture. The Fifth Schedule also makes the states responsible for promoting the educational and economic interests of the tribals and to protect them from social injustice and exploitation. The Central Government provides special financial assistance to the states under Article 275 for implementing schemes for the development of scheduled tribes. Tribal development policy under the Eighth Plan (1992-97) and the approach paper for the Ninth Five Year Plan stress people's initiative and participation as key elements in the development process and in protecting the interests of the tribals. High priority has been accorded to elimination of their exploitation and removal of all forms of oppression. Today, the tribal majority areas, which overlap with the country's major forest areas, are also areas with the highest concentrations of poverty.

DEMOGRAPHIC TRENDS

Madhya Pradesh: MP has the largest tribal population in the country with the STs comprising 23.27% of the state's population in 1991. The percentage of both the scheduled tribe and scheduled caste population in MP has increased during the last two decades (from 20.1% in 1971 to 23.3 in 1991 for the ST population, and 13.1% to 14.5% for the SC population) due to their relatively higher fertility rates. In 1991, the fertility rate of the state's SC population was 4.71, of the ST population 4.05 and that of the remaining population 3.76.

No separate data is available on key demographic parameters for the tribal population. Average life expectancy in Surguja district is 51.9 years. The crude birth rate ranges from 32 to 36 per thousand females in the two districts.

Bihar: According to the 1991 census, the total tribal population in Bihar was 6,616,914 (7.7% of the state population). 91% of the state's tribal population is concentrated in the 18 districts of south Bihar out of which the tribals constitute the majority only in 3 districts-Gumla, Lohardaga and West Singhbhum. The tribals are predominantly rural (93%) in spite of the fact that the level of urbanization in the region is 20.3% compared to 13% for the state as a whole. The density of population of the state as a whole is 497 whereas the density of population of the ST areas is 273.

In contrast to Madhya Pradesh, the fertility rate of the tribal population in Bihar at 3.42 is the lowest in the state compared to that of 3.95 among the SCs and 4.06 among the general population. The proportion of the ST population declined by over one full percentage point in 20 years.

Scheduled Tribes in the Study Area

The area studied in both the states has a combination of a variety of tribes and occupational artisan castes which have lived in a symbiotic relationship for a few hundred years. The tribes in the area belong to two linguistic groups. One group speaks the Austro-Asiatic or Mundari group of languages and includes the Santhal, Ho and Munda. The other group of tribes speaks a language of the Dravidian group-this includes the Oraon, Chero and Gond. The tribes themselves range from surviving remnants of almost pure hunter-gatherers among the 'Primitive Tribal Groups' (PTGs) to the settled agriculturist tribes like the Santhal, Ho, Munda, Oraon and Gond. However, until today, even the agricultural tribes do a considerable amount of gathering and all tribes share a historically strong collectivism in economic activities.

Madhya Pradesh: No recent data are available on the population by tribe for the programme blocks in MP. However, according to the 1961 census data, three main tribes, namely Gond, Oraon and Kanwar predominate in the three districts, accounting for more than 80% of their total tribal population. The main tribal groups in the three districts are:

- Raigarh/Jashpur: Oraon, Kanwar, Gond, Nagwanshi, Sawara, Kharia, Korwa, Baiga and Birhor
- Surguja: Gond, Oraon, Kanwar, Nagesia, Korwa, Baiga, Binjhwar

Bihar/Jharkhand: 30 tribes have been notified as scheduled tribes in Bihar. The most numerous STs are the Santhal, Oraon, Munda, Ho, Kharwar, Kharia and Bhumij which constitute about 86% of the total tribal population of the state. The major STs in the Bihar programme districts are:

- Ranchi: Oraon, Munda, Bhumij, Bedia (in Angara Block only), Mahali, Lohra and Kharia;
- East and West Singhbum: Santhal, Ho, Bhumij, Bathudi, Munda and Oraon.

Primitive Tribal Groups

Madhya Pradesh: 7 Scheduled Tribes have been recognized as `Primitive Tribal Groups' in MP These are: Pahari Korwa, Baiga, Avujhmariya, Bhariya, Kamar, Sahariya and Birhor. The MP government has set up separate development agencies, registered as autonomous societies, for each of the PTGs excepting the Birhors.

The PTG development agencies devote funds, in addition to those available for STs in general, exclusively for the PTGs. Their basic strategy for promoting more focused development of the PTGs is to form clusters of 4 to 5 PTG villages and make teams of officials from the revenue, rural development, education and the tribal welfare departments responsible for each cluster.

Bihar: Nine scheduled tribes have been classified as PTGs in Bihar: Asur, Birhor, Birjia, Korwa, Parhaiya, Savar, Hill Kharia, Mal Paharia and Sauria Paharia. Their total population is estimated at about 190,000 persons. The Birhor population in the study area is only 210 of which 190 live in only two villages in Angara block. There is no separate development agency for the PTGs in Bihar.

MIGRATION

Madhya Pradesh: Information collected by this mission, as well as by the PRAs and Non-Timber Forest Products (NTFPs) marketing study, suggests very low rates of migration from some of the programme blocks in MP. According to the BDO of Dharamjaigarh block for example, barely 50 families from the entire block migrate seasonally due to the availability of different NTFPs from the forests most of the year.

This was despite the fact that out of the 24,000 families below the poverty line in the 1996-97 survey, as many as 7000 (29%) were landless. In Odgi block, however, all the able-bodied persons in some villages migrate and return only just prior to the onset of the rains. The more general pattern in the block is that one or several members of half to one-third of the households in each village migrate for 3 to 4 months in the dry season.

Bihar: Although no precise information is available for the study area, the Chotanagpur Plateau is known to have high rates of migration, including to distant states such as Punjab and to Delhi. The PRAs done in Bihar came across seasonal migration particularly among the PTGs1.

SEX RATIOS

Madhya Pradesh. A striking demographic feature of the study area is the significantly higher female to male ratio compared to the all India ratio of 927 and the MP state ratio of 931 females per 1000 males (see Table below). Sex ratios among the STs in the programme blocks in Surguja district range from 950 (Odgi) to 985-6 (Mainpat, Lundra and Udaipur).

The relatively low sex ratio among the tribals in Odgi block is surprising due to the reportedly high levels of migration from the block. In Raigarh/Jaspur districts, all the programme blocks have over 1000 females per 1000 males ranging from 1003 (Bagicha) to 1028 (Manora). With almost no migration from Dharamjaigarh block, a female to male ratio of 1016 is again striking probably indicating the superior status of tribal women in the area.

Table. Sex Ratio (Females/1000 Males) in the Study Area in MP

District	Block	Sex Ratio (females/1000 males)		
		Total Population	SC	ST
Surguja		956	957	975
	Udaipur	976	982	986
	Shankargarh	972	960	974
	Odgi	951	936	950
	Mainpat	971	945	985
	Lundra	975	967	985
	Kusmi	973	975	977
Raigarh/Jaspur		1004	999	1020
	Bagicha	986	943	1003
	Manora	1012	921	1028
	Dharamjaigarh	1004	982	1016
	Pathalgaon	1002	999	1020
MP		931		
All India		927		

(Source: 1991 Census data)

Bihar. The female-male ratio among the tribal population in Bihar is again quite favourable compared to that for the state as a whole reflecting the relatively better status of women in tribal society. However, there was a significant decline even in the tribal sex ratio during the last decade as evident from the following Table.

Table. Female-Male Ratio in Bihar (Females/1000 males)

	Total Population	SC	ST	Non SC/ST
1981	946	966	993	937
1991	911	914	971	905

Source: Bihar Formulation report, taken from Basu, S.K, Health Status of Tribal Women in Social Change 23(4) p22.

In the study area in Bihar, excepting for Angara block, which has a lower sex ratio of 966 than the state ratio of 971 for the ST population, the ST sex ratio in all the other blocks is higher than the state average.

Excepting for Goelkera block with 974 females/1000 males, the sex ratio in the other 4 blocks in West Singhbhum ranges from 1002 (Sonua) to 1033 in Khuntpani. Unlike the study area in MP, the male adverse sex ratio in these 4 blocks could partly be due to their having a higher rate of male migration.

LITERACY

Madhya Pradesh: Literacy rates among the tribal population in the study area are very low, particularly among women. Overall, both ST male and female literacy rates in Raigarh/Jaspur districts are significantly higher than the literacy rates in Surguja district. ST male literacy in the programme blocks ranges from 17% (Odgi and Mainpat) to 39% (Manora).

ST female literacy ranges from as low as 4.3% (Odgi) to 23% (Manora). (see Table below). Literacy rates among the PTGs are even lower-barely 5% among the Pahari Korwas and almost nil amongst the women. Although the government has built residential schools for them, Pahari Korwa children tend to leave them and run away.

Table. Literacy Rates in the Study Area-MP

Name of Dist/Block	SC		ST		Total		No. of House-holds	Average size househ old
	M	F	M	F	M	F		
Raigarh District/Jaspur[2]	**41.0**	**14.3**	**37.5**	**16.3**	**45.8**	**21.7**	**226292**	**5**
Bagicha	31.3	10.1	33.2	16.6	34.9	16.6	24900	5
Manora	35.9	14.2	39.4	23.1	39.1	21.1	8694	6
Dhrmjaigarh	26.9	9.4	27.3	6.8	31.4	10.0	29872	5
Pathalgaon	35.5	11.5	31.6	10.7	34.9	12.7	25657	6
District Surguja	**28.8**	**10.1**	**23.4**	**7.1**	**33.5**	**13.7**	**368799**	**5.6**
Udaipur	17.1	5.1	22.5	6.0	24.2	7.7	10745	5
Kusmi	27.5	8.2	27.7	10.1	30.3	11.5	15308	5
Shankargarh	28.9	8.4	27.8	9.5	31.9	12.1	10357	5
Odgi	17.7	3.1	17.2	4.3	23.2	6.4	11056	5
Mainpat	40.2	10.4	17.4	5.4	22.7	8.2	10118	5
Lundra	23.2	6.9	20.2	5.6	25.6	8.6	15703	5

Source: 1991 Census Data

Bihar. Literacy among the tribal population at 23.6% in 1991 continues to be less than half that of for the total population of the state (52.2%) although it has increased fourfold over the last four decades (see Table below). While the state male literacy is 64.1%, the tribal male literacy is 32.5%. The tribal female literacy rate is particularly low at 14.5% compared to 29.3% for the total female population.

Table. Literacy Rates in Bihar

	Total Population			Tribal Population		
	T	M	F	T	M	F
1961	23.95	34.37	12.90	7.99	13.04	2.89
1971	29.48	39.52	18.70	10.89	17.09	4.58
1981	36.23	46.89	24.82	16.35	24.52	8.04
1991	52.21	64.13	29.29	23.63	32.50	14.50

Source: Bihar formulation report.

Both the male and female literacy rates in all the programme blocks are significantly lower than the literacy rates for the state as a whole. Male literacy in all but 2 of the programme blocks (Tonto 24.7%, Goelkera 29%) is higher than the state ST male literacy of 32.5%. Rajnagar block has the highest male literacy (44.2%). Female literacy, however, is lower than the state ST female literacy rate of 14.5% in all the programme blocks ranging from 5.9% (Tonto) to 13.9% (Rajnagar) (see Table below).

Table. Literacy and Sex Ratio in the Programme Blocks in Bihar

DST/Block	Literacy rate			Sex Ratio	
	Total	Male	Female	Total	ST Population
Ranchi					
Angara	24.1	37.7	10.0	963	966
Arki	21.9	34.3	9.5	987	988
West Singhbhum					
Goelkera	19.1	29.0	9.1	979	974
Tonto	15.3	24.7	5.9	1004	1005
Khuntpani	24.4	37.6	11.5	1025	1033
Sonua	27.0	40.3	13.4	985	1002
Rajnagar	29.1	44.2	13.9	986	1015
East Singhbhum					
Dumaria	23.8	35.7	11.6	980	997

Source: 1991 Census Data.

Literacy rates also vary among different tribes. In 1981, the Kharias had the highest literacy rate among the STs followed by the Oraons and the Mundas. These tribal groups have also adopted Christianity to a greater extent. Literacy among the PTGs was the lowest, ranging from 5.7% among the Birhors to 7.6% among the Mal Maharias. Literacy among the PTG female population in 1981 was about 2.5%.

HEALTH STATUS

The most common diseases among tribal communities are parasitic infections, diarrhoea, dysentery, skin diseases, respiratory infections, whooping cough and measles. Serious diseases such as tuberculosis, leprosy and malaria are also common in the study areas. Health facilities do not reach them because the norms prescribed by the State Governments for establishing Primary Health Centres and Health Sub-Centres are inappropriate for a dispersed population in small settlements in inaccessible areas. When health facilities happen to be available, most tribal villagers can neither pay the doctor nor pay for the medicines.

Tribal women's health is at risk during their reproductive years. Around 68 % of pregnant and lactating women suffer from anemia. Around 72 % of all births are attended by untrained traditional birth attendants (dais). Of particular interest, the maternal mortality rate is reported to be around 2 per 1000 live births compared to the national average of 4.4 per 1000 live births.

In interior villages with good forest cover, the communities rely on their traditional herbal medicine practices. In mixed villages, adoption of allopathic treatment has become a major source of indebtedness. Women members of Self Help Groups reported that they borrow from their savings group for health care; others obtained loans from money lenders.

The prevalent nutritional disorders are anemia and avitaminosis with the associated common deficiency diseases of a) angular conjunctivitis and angular stomatitis and pellagra, all assumed to be caused by riboflavin deficiency; b) night blindness and skin dryness or roughness attributed to vitamin A deficiency; c) endemic goitre, the principal aetiological factor of which is iodine deficiency.

The children portray a classic picture of chronic malnutrition with lower size, weight and height, for their age. This is undoubtedly related to the poor nutritional status of women, with an inter-generation transmission of malnutrition resulting in the very high incidence of low birth weight in India. 60% of the pre-school children are underweight and 25% severely underweight4. Pre-school children are the weakest section of the population. Mortality rates for ST children under five was 136 in Bihar and 167 in MP.

SETTLEMENT PATTERNS

Topography, socio-cultural characteristics, livelihood systems and to some extent, historical factors have shaped the settlement patterns in the study area. In terms of size and density, the settlements may be characterized as (i) small and scattered (only 10 to 15 houses), (ii) medium sized compact or dispersed (up to 100 houses in 1 to 3 or 4 hamlets) and (iii) larger usually more compact settlements.

Revenue villages in Bihar tend to be smaller than those in MP: 67% of the villages in the former have less than 500 inhabitants, compared to 39% in MP, where 56% of the population lives in villages of 500 to 2 000 inhabitants. The more compact and larger settlements tend to be in the plains and are inhabited by the more agriculturally advanced tribes. A revenue village may have between 2 to 7-8 `natural' villages consisting of settlements at considerable distance from each other. Most revenue villages do not represent social units of organization nor do they function as collective units of decision-making.

PTG settlements are primarily found in remote, forested and hilly tracts with some villages having only 10 to 15 houses5. The Birhors make their tandas in isolated patches with large gaps between two tandas to ensure that each community has adequate forest area for hunting and gathering. Pahari Korwa settlements often lack permanency as the entire settlement is abandoned if a number of deaths take place in the same neighbourhood6. The settlements may be of a single ethnic group or of several STs and castes. Traditional PTG settlements were uni-ethnic but subsequent to their resettlement outside forest areas, they often comprise hamlets within larger, mixed villages.

LOCAL LEVEL INSTITUTIONS

Traditional Institutions: The settled tribes in the study area have at least two levels of traditional leadership-within the village and for a cluster of villages of the clan for dealing with inter-village issues and disputes. Some of them also have a third and higher leadership level for addressing issues confronting the larger community. In almost all the settled tribes, the posts of the traditional leaders are hereditary often reserved for the male lineage of the `original reclaimers' of the land. The traditional village assembly has virtually been an all-male institution with women provided access only under highly exceptional circumstances.

PTGs: By virtue of their dependence on foraging, and the nature of collectivism and cooperation it requires, the social institutions of PTGs are the least hierarchical to facilitate consensual decision-making. In the absence of any attachment to private property, gender relations have been particularly egalitarian among the PTGs. Birhor settlements have traditionally had a council of elders composed of all elders of the group, both male and female. Regular political participation by women in the village council has also been reported in the case of the Korwa, a tribe that has only recently come into settled agriculture.

An overview of the present status of traditional village institutions in the study area in both states indicates the following patterns:

* The tradition of taking collective decisions based on consensus among most communities is still strong, particularly in the more remote villages.
* While in some cases traditional/hereditary leaders are still respected, in others they are being replaced by a new generation of young and educated leaders who have gained the community's respect and trust.
* In more heterogeneous communities, where socio-economic stratification and differentiation within tribals has increased, the new leadership represents the economically better off sections interested in increasing their political power.
* Within this pattern, small numbers of educated tribal women leaders are also beginning to emerge, in part, due to the reservation of one third seats for women in

PRIs. There is considerable openness to creating institutional space for women to start participating in community affairs.

* Traditional institutions continue to perform a number of regulatory functions within villages besides mobilizing the community for undertaking tasks of common interest when required. These have become weakest near the urban towns.

Modern Institutions: By far the single most pervasive modern village institution introduced in post independence India has been the Gram Panchayat as the lowest rung of local government. Intended to put into practice Mahatma Gandhi's vision of gram swaraj (village self rule) the Gram Panchayat effectively reconstructed the village for administrative convenience. Superimposition of statutory Panchayats in tribal areas has had many adverse impacts on their self governing traditional institutions. Concentration of power in the elected Panchayat Pradhans, combined with a lack of transparency and accountability in their functioning, slowly converted many panchayats into centres of corruption, political manipulation and factional rivalry.

During the last 10 to 15 years, with increasing recognition of the importance of people's participation for increasing the effectiveness of development interventions, an extensive array of `people's' institutions have been created in the villages for the implementation of sectoral programmes. These include joint forest management (JFM) committees being set up by the Forest Department, education committees by the Education Department, watershed associations and committees by the DRDA, water and health committees by the Public Health Department, water users association by the Irrigation Department, and Mahila Mandals (women's associations) by the Women and Child Department. Under a number of special programmes such as the Bihar Education Programme, selected village women are trained as animators to organize women not only for accessing literacy but also for dealing with their other problems.

New Institutions Promoted by NGOs: Many NGOs have also been promoting a variety of new institutions within villages. Their nature and tenor varies with the ideology and perspective of the concerned NGO.

Some NGO-promoted village institutions have traits similar to those promoted by government departments while others focus on leadership development and community mobilization. Some NGOs are also providing support to self-initiated forest protection associations of the villagers. Training and supporting cadres of village animators for organizing and mobilizing predominantly male youth groups is another NGO focus.

Among the more dynamic new institutions being promoted by NGOs, although on a limited scale and only by a few NGOs, are women's associations for advocacy and local action on issues affecting women's lives and self-help groups (SHGs) engaged in savings and credit and/or income generation activities.

LIVELIHOOD SYSTEMS IN THE STUDY AREA

Livelihood systems in the study area are primarily dependent on various combinations of agriculture, forests and labour. Livestock and fish rearing are closely integrated in the farming systems. There are also a number of artisanal castes and tribal groups who depend either on providing services to the community or on small-scale processing and marketing. The traditional livelihood system of the PTGs consisted of shifting cultivation, hunting and gathering forest foods and other produce.

They are undergoing a painful process of enforced transition to settled cultivation outside the forests. Although many still depend to some extent on hunting and forest products, these are no longer their main source of livelihood. Instead they are grappling with survival on poor quality non-forest lands without agricultural implements. Women's work is regarded as crucial for the survival of tribal households in terms of provisioning for food, income earning, as well as management of resources.

Typology of Livelihood Systems

The tribal livelihood systems identified in the study area can be classified according to the degree of dependence on forest resources.

Forest dependent upland systems, usually located in upper watersheds where most PTG Villages are also located, are estimated to represent about 20% of the study area. Communities in these watersheds live in small, scattered settlements located near or within reserve or protected forests. PTGs in such areas are under transition from pure forest dependence to a mixed forest/agriculture/wage labour system due to resettlement, and declining forest productivity. Characteristics include a continuing dependence, often unsustainable, on harvesting of firewood and some NTFPs such as roots/tubers, bamboo, tendu, sal leaves and fibre collected for consumption or sale. Limited permanent or shifting cultivation is practiced within a defined village forest territory, providing food security for 2 to 4 months. Small stock consists of poultry, pigs and goats which are sold when cash is needed. In Bihar, there is substantial reliance on seasonal migration for wage work outside the village (in brick kilns, mining or road construction) to supplement incomes. Headloading is often an important source of income, particularly for women: according to the PRA study in Bihar, 90% of the households in such villages were practicing headloading as a survival strategy, an activity primarily undertaken by women.

Mixed systems, located in middle watersheds, comprise about 65% of the study area. These are partially hilly areas with communities having lesser dependence on forest than the former and in place of this there is added reliance on agriculture. Farming is mainly single crop with some paddy and vegetable cultivation. Some farmers may own bullocks and use manure for maintaining soil fertility. Food security extends to 3 to 4 months. Access is interrupted at certain times of the year and so market orientation is somewhat limited with a greater focus on subsistence production. Migration can involve up to 50% of households in this system.

Lowland systems, located in lower watersheds and covering about 15% of the study area. These communities extend into the lower plains and may have relatively little forest access. They tend to be more multi-ethnic, have smaller but more intensively farmed landholdings and own more bullocks. Double cropping is more common and, where irrigation is available, even a third crop may be grown. There is a greater reliance on paddy, vegetable cultivation occurs year round and overall food security can extend to 5 to 7 months. A much greater market orientation is present due to year-round market access. Many fields may already be bunded as the terrain is generally flatter and there is better information about water management techniques. In general, farming has been carried out for a longer period and this is demonstrated in greater productivity per hectare. Distant migration may be less prevalent with greater availability of wage work locally.

COMPONENTS OF LIVELIHOOD SYSTEMS

Land Holding Patterns: In Bihar 56% of the farmers operate an average of 0.4 ha whilst 71% of the holdings are less then 2 ha; the average of holdings with less than 2 ha is 0.6 ha. In Madhya Pradesh about 51% of the cultivators are marginal farmers (average holding 0.4 ha), accounting for only 11% of the cultivated area. About 20% of the farmers are small farmers with an average size of 1.5 ha accounting for 16% of the cultivated area. The rest of the farmers (23%) cultivate 73% of the land. These figures, however, refer to all holdings in the study blocks, including those of non-tribals. Broadly speaking, holding patterns of tribals tend to be more egalitarian and holding sizes smaller. About 75% of the tribal households have firm title to their land. Land tenure issues mainly concern `encroached' forest land. Information about the extent of landlessness is not readily available except for the PTGs in Surguja district.

PTGs: 55.3% of Pahari Korwas in the study blocks are landless. As the PTGs never had titles to the forests in which they traditionally subsisted, `landlessness' among them is a product of delegitimization of their traditional livelihood system. Although the government is allotting them non-forest land, it is normally unproductive and many remain landless or lack proper land titles. Even if they have titles, the actual possession is often in the hands of other tribals or non-tribals with the land owners working as labourers on their own land. Many PTGs sell off the land allotted to them to people of other tribes at low rates and revert to their traditional life style of living in the forest.

Agricultural Production Patterns: Agriculture in the study area is predominantly rainfed and monocropped: only about 8% of the cultivated land in the Bihar study area and 4% in MP is under irrigation. Less than 25% of the gross-cropped area is double cropped. Paddy is the major crop accounting for about 60 to 70% of the cultivated land during the kharif season, with productivity ranging from 450 kg to 1100 kg/ha. The other crops are maize, a variety of millets13 sorghum, wheat, barley, pulses and oil seeds. Food grains occupy about 95% of the cropped area. Paddy, maize, millets, arhar, niger and groundnut are the important kharif crops while the main crops grown in the rabi season are wheat, oilseeds (rapeseed, mustard, linseed, groundnut, pigeon pea and niger), pulses (lentil and gram), and vegetables. Horticulture is little developed in the study area with the present area under fruits, vegetables, and spices accounting for only about 2.5% of the cultivated area. Vegetable cultivation is picking up very fast. These are preferably grown on Bari land (homestead). Women participate in all agricultural operations excepting ploughing and sowing of rice seed, contributing between 70 to 80% of the total labour.

Household Food Security: The extent to which the tribals are able to meet their food requirements from agriculture is determined by the type of land they own, the size of the holdings and the size of the household. The PRAs as well as the seasonality analysis done by the mission agronomists, indicate a declining role of agriculture in household food security which lasts for 2 to 6 months of the year for the majority of farming households. It is estimated that average households in upland systems are only able to meet 20 to 40% of their food requirements; those in the middle system 30 to 40% and those in lowland systems between 50 to 70% of their needs. Food insecurity peaks in the post-sowing monsoon period (August-September) and again around March when the kharif harvest has been exhausted. In the past, most tribals were able to cover most of the shortfall with foods gathered from the forests. Forest degradation and curtailed forest access has reduced the availability of natural foods on which they depended compelling the tribals, especially those in the upland and mixed systems, to depend more and more on purchased foods to meet their minimum survival needs. Impoverished villagers have to choose between migrating for wage work or resorting to unsustainable harvesting of firewood for survival income14. Many tribals have become caught in a debt trap because of the precariousness of their food security situation.

Forests in the Livelihood System. In extent, forests cover approximately 28% of the geographical area of the program districts in Bihar and 46% in MP. Forests supply timber, fodder, fuelwood and a large number of Non-Timber Forest Products. Despite forest degradation, NTFPs contribute significantly to the economy of the study area. Almost all households living in the forest belt depend upon collection of NTFPs for consumption and sale. Mahua and tendu leaf are economically the two most important items, both primarily collected by women.

According to the NTFP study done in MP for the reformulation mission, as many as 50 NTFPs are still gathered from the forests in the study area. Income per household (including an allowance for the value of non-marketed NTFPs) ranges from just over Rs.2000 to more than Rs.5000 and includes collection activities (e.g. edible plants, tendu leaf, seeds, etc.) and processing activities (e.g. basket-making, rope-making, de-seeding, etc.). This is in addition to the value of grazing, firewood and timber for house construction derived from the forests.

GENDER ROLES IN FOREST USE

Among the PTGs such as Birhor, Pahari Korwa and Savar, women play important roles in (a) food gathering from the forests; (b) rope-making from the bark of trees and sabai grass

(Birhor); (c) honey collection; (d) herbal medicinal plant collection and processing, sale; (e) hunting and trapping; (f) basket-making; (g) shifting cultivation; (h) labour; and (i) fishing. Among the Birhors, sale or barter of rope in exchange for cash or grain is the exclusive work of women.

Food gathering is a vital economic activity even for women of the settled tribes. Various types of roots, stems, leaves, fruits, flowers and mushrooms are collected through the year. Roots and stems are the most important forest foods which constitute a major part of their diet. Leaves, vegetables and mushrooms are often consumed as complete meals.

The extent of women's income from NTFPs in the study area can be gauged from the fact that in Surguja district, Rs.14 crores are paid as wages for Tendu leaf collection annually, a product primarily gathered by women. In Surguja's east forest division in which 3 of the programme blocks (Kusmi, Lundra and Shankargarh) fall, Rs.4 crores are paid as wages for Tendu leaf collection and Rs.2 crores for Sal seed collection annually. Another Rs.2 to 3 crores are earned annually through the collection of other NTFPs in the unorganized sector.

LIVESTOCK

Livestock raising is an important component of the tribal culture and of the production systems and is fully integrated with crop production. Cattle and buffaloes provide draft power, manure, play an important role in threshing operations and livestock constitutes a cash reserve for times of distress. Traditionally, livestock is grazed on common and wasteland and also in the forest during the monsoon season.

Once produce is harvested, the stubbles and volunteer grasses become the main grazing areas throughout the rest of the year. Overall 70-90% of households in the programme districts in MP own livestock excluding poultry (mainly cattle and pigs) and the proportion increases to over 90% if poultry is included. Livestock is mostly of local breed. Tribal communities generally do not milk the cattle and milk is not a traditional part of their diet.

DEPENDENCE ON LABOUR

Most tribal households depend on wage labour to eke out a living. Dependence on wage labour is much higher in villages away from forests, (for over half the year) when food from their own lands is not available. Wage work is done both within the village and in neighbouring towns. Within the village, it is mostly agricultural work whereas outside, the villagers work in brick kilns and as unskilled construction labour.

Women's participation in wage work is equal to that of the men. However, agricultural wages paid to women are almost always lower than those paid to men. (refer Table below15). Landless SC women are often the poorest and most dependent on wages. In many tribal villages, agricultural wage-rates are fixed in Gram Sabha meetings based on the paying capacity of the landowners.

The tradition of keeping women's wages lower than those of men, while sustaining the low return agricultural economy, also means that it relies heavily on poor women's cheap labour.

Table. Range of Women and Men's Wage Rates in the Study Area

Place	Women (Rs.)	Men (Rs)
Agricultural wages, local		
Ambikapur block	20-25	25-50
Kusmi block	25	30
Dharamjaigarh	4 tami rice	same as
(Rathia Kanwar)	+ 1 meal	for women
Pathalgaon block (Gond Majhi)	20	30
Pathalgaon block (mixed)	15	25-30
Tonto block (Ho)	12+2 snacks	20+2 snacks
Government wage rates		
Forest Dept.(MP)	55.19	55.19
JRY, Surguja dist.	42.50	42.50

Indebtedness: According to the rural financial sector study conducted for this mission, 58% of the tribal households in Bihar and 47% in Madhya Pradesh were indebted: the estimated average debt per indebted household was INR 2917 in Bihar and INR 5918 in Madhya Pradesh. Degree of indebtedness was found highest amongst marginal farmers in Bihar (75% of the sample) and landless labourers in MP (52%). In MP, around 67% of borrowing was for productive purposes and 33% for consumption. Borrowing for repayment of old debt was also a major feature of borrowing for non-productive purposes. Of the total borrowings, about 67% in Bihar and 50% in MP was from informal sources.

Availing of Loans: A major reason for women not being able to avail IRDP loans is their not having any land or property which can be used as collateral by the banks. Even the studies done on rural finance for the mission found that women had next to no access to the formal credit institutions. In the study area in Madhya Pradesh, only about 13% of the sample households and in Bihar, only 11% households had availed of loans from formal credit institutions in women's names.

SOCIAL AND ECONOMIC STATUS OF TRIBAL WOMEN

Gender Relations in Tribal Culture

It is widely recognized that tribal women enjoy a better status within their own communities than women in mainstream Indian society. There are few restrictions on their mobility. Women have considerable freedom of choice in the selection of marriage partners and tribal cultures have liberal norms related to divorce and remarriage by women.

Due to their important role in the agriculture-cum-forest based tribal economies, women have traditionally enjoyed respect as economically-valued members of their communities. This is reflected in the tradition of bride price instead of dowry among most tribal communities. A major indicator of tribal women's better status even in the study area is the highly favourable tribal female to male ratio in almost all the blocks compared to those of other communities.

Among the settled agricultural tribes, however, there have been two crucial areas of gender inequality by tradition-property rights and political participation. Among most agricultural tribes in the study area, property, particularly land, passes through the male lineage and under customary law, women do not have inheritance rights to land. Under Section 3 of the Indian Succession Act of 1925, the State Government of Bihar has exempted most STs in the state from the purview of normal succession laws. Matters of inheritance and rights to property among these tribes are governed by their customary laws.. The second important area of gender inequality among the settled tribes has been that of political participation with women being excluded from traditional community institutions. The second important area of gender inequality among the settled tribes has been that of political participation with women being excluded from traditional community institutions.

Women of even settled tribes, however, have traditionally had control over their own income from wages or the sale or processing of NTFPs that they collect from common lands and forests. To some extent, this has countered the gender inequality in property rights by providing women a certain degree of economic independence and greater control over household food security. However, as discussed below, this position of tribal women is under threat of rapid erosion.

GENDER ROLES, KNOWLEDGE AND TABOOS IN AGRICULTURE

The majority of labour for agricultural production (between 70-80% by different estimates) in the study area is provided by women (see Table below for rice cultivation), yet government, and even most NGO interventions in the agricultural sector are generally blind to women's role in the farming system. Demonstrations and training in new technology, distribution of seeds and fertilizer as well as loans and subsidies are being targeted only at men16. The same is the case with the schemes of the horticulture and animal husbandry departments with all fruit plants, ducks, goats and chicken being distributed primarily to men.

Such an acute gender imbalance in access to new agricultural knowledge and resources created by such interventions is tending to undermine women's traditionally respected role in the production system. There is not a single woman agricultural extension worker in the programme districts in MP. A recent directive of the state government, however, has reserved one-third of future recruitment of agricultural extension workers for women.

Table. Gender Roles in Rice Cultivation

Activity	Performed by		Remarks
	Men	Women	
Carrying manure to the fields		*	
Ploughing	*		Ploughing is forbidden for women.
Breaking mud clods		*	
Sowing rice	*		Women are forbidden from sowing rice seed.
Transplanting		*	
Hoeing/weeding		*	
Harvesting	*	*	
Carrying to threshing ground	*	*	
Threshing with bullocks	*	*	
Cleaning the threshed crop		*	
Packing main crop for storage	*		
Seed selection and storage		*	
Selling (if surplus available)	*	*	Small quantities may be sold by women. Sale of larger quantities is either done through consultation or by the men.

Age-old taboos also forbid women to perform certain tasks. These include ploughing, sowing the seed of the main rice crop17 (although the backbreaking work of transplanting paddy is considered exclusively women's work) and tiling the roof of a house. The women are liable to social punishment if they violate any of the three taboos. In essence, these prevent women from gaining independent capability in agricultural production or in acquiring shelter.

There were no such taboos for women of the foraging tribes. Seed broadcasting under shifting cultivation was done by women and women participated equally in house construction. Ploughing was absent in any case. With many of the PTGs shifting to settled agriculture, their women are rapidly internalizing the gender roles and practices of the settled tribes.

CHANGING ATTITUDES TO WOMEN'S POLITICAL PARTICIPATION

Considerable attitudinal changes towards women's traditional exclusion from political participation at both the community and higher levels are evident among the settled tribes. Three major processes have contributed to such change. Perhaps the most significant ones have been the political struggles of the tribals themselves. During the most dynamic phase of the Jharkhand Mukti Morcha's movement in the mid-1970s in the Chotanagpur plateau, women were encouraged to form women's associations in every village to fight against the 'internal' enemies of polygamy and rampant alcoholism among men to revitalize tribal society. Large numbers of women were active participants in this struggle.

Secondly, under the ambit of different government programmes, mahila mandals (women's associations) have been formed in many villages as forums for reaching development inputs to women. Women's associations were also formed during the total literacy campaign for increasing literacy among women. Under the Bihar Education Programme, which is now being extended to all districts of the state, trained women animators organize women's associations for literacy and dealing with their other problems. Under the Government of India's DWCRA (Development of Women and Children in Rural Areas) scheme, women's groups are being organized in many villages for income generation activities. The reservation of one third seats for women in PRIs has had a visible impact in MP. Due to no panchayat elections having been held in Bihar for 19 years, such impact is less evident in Bihar. Other government programmes, such as JFM and Watershed Development, under which new village institutions are being promoted, are also encouraging women's participation in community affairs.

Lastly, there have been many NGO initiatives to organize and mobilize women. These include women's savings and credit groups, and advocacy groups for women's rights and against domestic violence.

Although uneven, the cumulative impact of all these interventions has increased acceptance of women's participation in government or NGO promoted groups and community institutions. The traditional male-only village assembly has either learnt to co-exist with such new institutions or has started to transform by accepting women in its ambit. Women still do not attend the traditional male gatherings unless specifically invited. When invited by the male leaders, they often turn up in large numbers. In the context of the continuing high levels of illiteracy among tribals, educated tribal women enjoy special respect in their communities and are gaining acceptance in leadership roles.

TRENDS OF CHANGE IN WOMEN'S RIGHTS

Despite women not having inheritance rights to land under customary law among most settled tribes, various social arrangements have existed to ensure adequate care of women in situations of widowhood, breakdown of marriage, single women and for families having only daughters.

Thus, widowed women acquired use rights to their husband's property for maintenance for life. On their death, the property passed into the hands of the husband's nearest male relatives. Both unmarried daughters and daughters who returned to their paternal homes due to breakdown of marriage, similarly acquired use rights in their paternal property for life maintenance. In the case of families having only daughters, sons-in-law could inherit their parental property if they agreed to settle in their wife's paternal village. Severe social sanctions for violation of these norms reduced the vulnerability of women in such situations.

The weakening of traditional institutions has reduced such traditional social protection enjoyed by tribal women. The rising value and scarcity of land are leading to a breakdown in women's maintenance rights. Several incidents of women inheriting land being labelled witches and being hounded out (occasionally even killed) by male relatives to grab the land, have been reported from the Jharkhand area. The worst sufferers in this category are widowed women in the age group of 55 and above.

During the field visits, it was found that unmarried daughters of Ho families are now allocated only one acre of their paternal land for life maintenance, while the rest is divided equally among the brothers, irrespective of the total size. Given the taboos against women ploughing, sowing and building roofs, such women remain dependent on their male relatives both for cultivating the land and for shelter. With many such women continuing to live with one of the brothers after the parents' death, their status and condition within such households needs to be understood better.

There were also indications that the number of daughters remaining unmarried may be increasing for a variety of reasons.

WOMEN HEADED AND WOMEN SUPPORTED HOUSEHOLDS

In most of the villages visited, an effort was made to identify the number of women headed and women supported households to understand their status and food security situation. In the limited time available it was difficult to communicate the concept of women supported households (with the man either away, sick or prone to excessive drinking), due to which the villagers only estimated the widows in their villages. Between 7 to 10%

of the households appeared to be headed by widowed women. The percentage of women supported households must be considerably higher in villages with rampant alcoholism and male migration. While in the case of some widows, land ownership had been transferred to their names, in others it had been transferred to their sons. Among the Gond Manjhi tribe in Pathalgaon, the widows now receive only 50% of their husband's land, the other half going to the woman's younger brother-in-law. In a mixed Oraon-Dehadi Korwa village, the tradition had changed to no land being transferred to the widow's name with all of it being given to the sons. In most cases, daughters inherited land only when there were no sons.

CONTROL OVER INCOME AND AGRICULTURAL PRODUCE

Traditionally, ownership and control over income earned through one's labour from non-private property strictly belonged to the person who expended the labour. Thus income from collection and processing/sale of NTFPs from forest lands belonged to the man, woman or child who had invested the labour in the activity.

In the case of produce or income from private land owned by the men, by and large the ownership rested with the land owner. This is most strictly observed among the Munda. Among the other tribes, although the ownership generally rests with the male `head' of the household, its management and control were shared by husband and wife. Due to tribal women's major role in trade and marketing, and having primary responsibility for household provisioning, they have also been the effective `managers' of household income and agricultural produce.

THREATS TO WOMEN'S INCOME AND STATUS

Women in all the villages visited, categorically stated that they kept and controlled their own income (usually from wages, NTFPs and petty processing/ trading). As far as the husband's income was concerned, while some said that even the husbands handed over their incomes to their wives for household maintenance, in other cases, it either depended on individual husbands or the men kept their income in their own hands (see Table below).

Table. Women's Control Over Income Within the Household

Village	Community	Management and Control Over Income
Charhat Nala (Kusmi block)	Nagesia	Women keep their earnings; Men keep theirs.
Barhnijharia (Ambikapur block)	Pando	Women keep their earnings. Men also give theirs to the women for management.
Sunna (Bagicha block)	Oraon, Nagesia, S.C.	Women keep their earnings; Men also may hand theirs to the women.
Karmi Tikra (Pathalgaon block)	Gond Majhi	Women keep their earnings. Men also give theirs to the women.
Ramsai (Tonto block)	Ho	Women keep their earnings, men also give theirs to them. Either can sell agricultural produce for meeting household expenses.

Women's ability to retain control over their incomes and their traditional status are being increasingly threatened by some of the following factors:

* *Alcoholism:* With increasing marginalization and alienation, excessive alcohol consumption has become widespread among tribal men. Not only do the men's incomes decline but they start snatching even the women's earnings. Resistance invites domestic violence and abuse. Household food security becomes a major casualty.
* *Migration and Bigamy:* In areas with high male migration, the men tend to bring other women back with them, throwing out their wives. With traditional

institutions for regulating such behaviour at the weakest in such areas, the issue of women's land and inheritance rights is acquiring a new dimension. Tribal women's land rights are also becoming an important issue with a minority of educated women gaining geographical and social mobility. A number of NGOs are working on the issue.

* Stereotype assumptions governing development interventions. As the majority of government programmes continue to target only men as the presumed `heads' of households, traditional gender relations, characterized by greater balance and complementarity, are being affected.

STATE GOVERNMENT POLICIES FOR WOMEN

MP is one of the few Indian states which has framed a state policy for women. Among other things, the policy advocates women's empowerment through increasing their access, ownership and control over productive assets, skills and resources and increasing their presence and participation in institutions at managerial and decision-making levels. Due to the important role of forests in local livelihood systems, the policy has a specific section on women and forests. This advocates ensuring that payment for NTFPs such as tendu leaf18 must be made directly to the women collectors, and that their membership of primary Tendu Leaf Cooperative Societies and representation in their managing committees should be increased and the proportion of women phad munshis19 increased to 50% by the turn of the century. New 'community' institutions also promoted by government have had some beneficial impact on creating space for women's participation in community affairs.

HOUSEHOLD TYPOLOGY, PERCEPTIONS AND PRIORITIES

Typology of Households

For this study, households were subdivided into four socio-economic strata:

* the poorest of the poor: nearly all the Primitive Tribal Groups, the landless households and the female headed/ supported households with young children;
* the very poor: nearly all the remote forest dependent villages practicing upland farming systems, all the other female headed households, all the marginal farmers independently of the production system, and some of the small farmers not having access to any lowland;
* the poor: most villages practicing mixed production systems and small farmer households having some fields in lowlands;
* the less poor: small farmer households and other farmers, especially those having access to lowland with an assured source of irrigation.

PERCEPTION OF POVERTY AND WELL BEING

During the PRA exercise, an attempt was made to understand, from the perspectives of tribal women and men, the dimensions of poverty and well being. Independently of the tribe, caste or gender, landlessness (or very small holdings), followed by dependency on wage labour emerged as the main indicators of poverty. Subsidiary ones, in descending order, were lack of (or few) livestock, not enough food from the farm, no access to drinking water and low levels of literacy.

Indicators of well being for men from settled tribes were: (i) assured source of water though construction of tanks, water management, and/or lift irrigation (ii) access to good supply of improved seeds, (iii) regular monthly income and (iv) having a school in the village. Settled women's perception of well being were: (i) food self-sufficiency, (ii) access to health and education, and (iii) having a large number of livestock.

Indicators of well being of men from PTG's were: (i) permanent rights to land, (ii) protection of crops from wild animals and (iii) easy access to NTFPs. For PTG women (i) having access to food throughout the year, (ii) good housing conditions and (iii) no consumption of alcohol by men emerged as indicators of well being.

PRIORITIES AT VILLAGE AND HOUSEHOLD LEVEL

According to the PRA exercise, water management (construction/rehabilitation of tanks and construction of check dams and other forms of community irrigation), emerged as the overwhelming priority of all sample villages. Land development support for the uplands and better roads were the other priority for males of settled tribes.

Priorities for women were: (i) availability and proximity of fuelwood and water, (ii) availability of good quality seeds, (iii) education and (iv) proximity of a public distribution shop.

Priorities for men from PTGs were: (i) permanent title to land; (ii) license to collect NTFP, (iii) availability of good quality seeds and (iv) bullocks for ploughing. For women from PTG tribes, priorities were: (i) local employment opportunities; (ii) education for children; (iii) access to a public distribution shop; (iv) availability of seeds, and (v) construction of a causeway on the stream to allow passage of people during the rainy season.

1. In a Birhor village in Angara block for example, the majority of households were found dependent on seasonal migration for several months each year.
2. The relatively higher literacy rates among the ST population in Raigarh/Jaspur districts compared to those in Surguja district are attributed to the work of Christian missionary organizations.
3. All information on health and nutrition is based on the 1992-93 NFHS (National Family Health Survey).
4. Underweight prevalence among pre-school children in Kerala is 28.5 % compared to 62.6 % in Bihar.
5. Poor nutrition, excessive alcohol consumption and the lack of safe drinking water and health facilities in their settlements due to their small, scattered and remote nature, makes the situation grave for the PTGs if they become afflicted by an infectious disease.
6. By tradition, the Pahari Korwas also abandon the house in which a death has taken place.

7. In the interior Mutu village in Manora block, the tradition of both the women and the men getting together to discuss village affairs was found to be intact. In addition, groups of neighbours were continuing to work collectively on each others' private lands for agricultural operations.

8. In a Ho village in Tonto block, a number of younger men, not related to the traditional leadership, had heard about the movement for tribal self rule (TSR) and had taken the initiative to form a village association to organize the villagers. 2 of the 9 members of the managing committee they had formed were women.

9. In a mixed tribal and caste village in Bagicha block, although the community spirit was still alive, considerable socio-economic stratification had developed within the village. Ghasi Scheduled Caste members of the community were landless and the poorest while four Muslim traders were engaged in money lending and an Oraon teacher had accumulated 50 acres of land.

10. In Dharamjaigarh block of Raigarh district, a `Samaj Panchayat' of 23 villages of the Rathia Kanwar community was being held. The woman chairperson of a village forest committee (VFC) had gone there to raise the issue of her daughter, married into another village, being made to do what she considered an unreasonably high amount of work by her in-laws.

11. The decision about the Lo Bir Sendra (annual hunt) among the Santhals, about transplanting and wage rates among the Hos and seasonal management of cattle grazing among most communities, continue to be taken in Gram Sabha meetings.

12. One NGO working in the study area in Bihar, has been facilitating the development of such village women's associations which take up cases related to women's land rights, promote collective action against alcoholism and domestic violence, support income generation through NTFP processing and increase awareness among

women about the legislation related to tribal self rule. Interestingly, initially they encountered strong resistance from traditional male leaders to women's active participation in the Gram Sabhas on grounds of its being against tribal `cultural traditions'.

13. Ragi (finger millet), Marua (Eleusine), Gundli (Panicum milare), pearl millet, other minor millets.
14. In the four villages within or near forests where PRAs were done in Bihar, as many as 91% of the total households were found dependent on collection and sale of firewood from the forests, an activity primarily done by women.
15. The mission came across only a couple of cases where the local wage rate for women and men was the same.
16. In Raigarh district, the only women beneficiaries were the minuscule minority of female landowners. The participation of women even in village-based training programmes was 1-5%. Only 3.5% of the beneficiaries of tank leases for fisheries in Raigarh district were women.
17. In the case of maize, however, the woman sows the seed walking behind the man on the plough. Women can also sow vegetables possibly due to vegetable cultivation being a recent introduction to the local cropping pattern.
18. Leaves of the Tendu tree, primarily collected by women and used for rolling cheap Indian cigarettes called Bidis are one of the economically most important NTFP in the study area. The annual turnover of the trade runs into many Rupees.
19. Local agents appointed for collecting tendu leaves on a commission basis.

BIBLIOGRAPHY

Aggarwal, L. B.: *The Harijans in Rebellion*, Bombay, Taraporewala and Sons, 1934.

Arvind, Sharma : *Women in World Religion,* New York Press, New York, 1990.

Azad, Maulana Abul Kalam: *India Wins Freedom*, New Delhi, Orient Longman, 1959.

Benjamin, J.: *Socio-religious Status of Girl Child in India,* New Delhi, Ashish Publishing, 1991.

Bhai, N.: *Harijan Women in Independent India*, Delhi, BR Publishing 1986

Bhasin, K., Menon, R. & Khan, N.S.: *Against All Odds: Essays on Women, Religion and Development from India and Pakistan*, Delhi, Isis International and Kali for Women 1994

Bhattarcharjea, Ajit: *Countdown to Partition: The Final Days*, New Delhi, HarperCollins, 1998.

Brasted, Howard: *Freedom, Trauma, Continuities: Northern India and Independence*. New Delhi, Sage Publications, 1998.

Calman, J.: *Toward Empowerment: Women and Politics in India*, Colorado, Westview Press, 1992.

Campbell-Johnson, Alan: *Mission with Mountbatten*, London, Hale, 1982.

Chandra Mowli, V.: *'Jogin'. Girl-Child Labour Studies*, New Delhi, Sterling 1992

Chandra, S.K.: *Development of Women Entrepreneurship in India. A Study of Public Policies and Programmes*, New Delhi, Mittal 1991

Chatterji, Joya: *Bengal Divided: Hindu Communalism and Partition, 1932-1947*, Cambridge, Cambridge UP, 1994.

Chopra, P. N.: *Towards Freedom: Documents on the Movement for Independence in India, 1937*. Delhi, Oxford UP, 1986.

Dak, T.M.: *Women and Work in Indian Society*, Delhi, Discovery, 1988.

Dixon-Mueller, R.: *Women's Work in Third World Agriculture*, Geneva, ILO, 1985.

Dube, L. & Palriwala, R.: *Structures and Strategies. Women, Work and Family*, New Delhi, Sage 1990.

Erikson, E. H.: *Childhood and Society*, New York, W. W. Norton, 1993.

Fine, M.: *Women with Disabilities: Essays in Psychology, Culture, and Politics*, Philadelphia, Temple University Press, 1988.

French, Patrick: *Liberty or Death: India's Journey to Independence and Division*, London, 1997.

Gilligan, C.: *In a Different Voice: Psychological Theory and Women's Development*, Cambridge, Harvard University Press, 1993.

Gilmartin, David: *Empire and Islam: Punjab and the Making of Pakistan*, London, Oxford UP, 1988.

Gupta, Shanti S.: *Varna, Castes and Scheduled Castes: A Documentation in Historical Perspective With a Classified Index to Scholarly Writings in Indian Journals (1890-1990)*, New Delhi, Concept Pub Co., 1991.

Hasan, Murhirul: *Legacy of a Divided Nation: India's Muslims Since Independence*, New Delhi, Oxford, 1997.

Hasan, Mushirul: *India's Partition: Process, Strategy and Mobilization*, New Delhi, Oxford UP, 1993.

Hasan, Mushirul: *Inventing Boundaries: Gender, Politics and the Partition of India*, Delhi, Oxford UP, 2000.

Hodson, H. V.: *The Great Divide: Britain-India-Pakistan*, Karachi, Oxford UP, 1993.

Jain, D.: *Women's Quest for Power*, Sahibabad, Vikas, 1980.

Jha, P. S.: *Kashmir, 1947: Rival Versions of History*, Delhi, Oxford UP, 1996.

Johnson, Alan: *Mission with Mountbatten*, London, Hale, 1982.

Jordan, J. V.: *Women's Growth in Diversity,* New York, Guilford Press, 1997.

Jumani, U.: *Dealing with Poverty. Self-employment for Poor, Rural Women,* London, Sage 1991.

Kaul, Rekha: *Caste, Class and Education: Politics of the Capitation Fee Phenomenon in Karnataka,* New Delhi, Sage Publications, 1993.

Kelles-Viitanen, A.: *Invisible Hands. Women in Home-based Production,* New Delhi, Sage, 1987.

Khan, N.S.: *Against All Odds: Essays on Women, Religion and Development from India and Pakistan,* Delhi, Isis International and Kali for Women 1994

Kitchlu, T.N.: *Widows in India,* New Delhi, Ashish, 1993.

Low, D. A. and Brasted, Howard: *Freedom, Trauma, Continuities: Northern India and Independence.* New Delhi, Sage Publications, 1998.

Mathur, B.B.: *Women and Depressed Class Population in India,* Allahabad, Chugh, 1994.

Menon, V. P.: *The Transfer of Power in India,* Bombay, Orient Longman, 1957.

Michel, A. A.: *The Indus Rivers: A Study of the Effects of Partition,* New Haven, Yale UP, 1967.

Moon, Penderel: *Divide and Quit,* Delhi, Oxford UP, 1998.

Mueller, R.: *Women's Work in Third World Agriculture,* Geneva, ILO, 1985.

Nair, Janaki: *Women and Law in Colonial India,* New Delhi, Kali, 1996.

Nanda, B.R.: *Indian Women. From Purdah to Modernity,* New Delhi, Vikas, 1976.

Otsea, K.: *Progress and Prospects: The Safe Motherhood Initiative 1987-1992,* Washington, D.C., World Bank, 1992.

Palriwala, R.: *Structures and Strategies. Women, Work and Family,* New Delhi, Sage 1990.

Panini, M.N.: *From the Female Eye. Accounts of Women Fieldworkers Studying their Own Communities,* Delhi, Hindustan, 1991.

Penderel, M.: *Divide and Quit*, Delhi, Oxford UP, 1998.

Philips, C. H. and Wainwright, M. D.: *The Partition of India: Policies and Perspectives 1935-47*, London, Allen and Unwin, 1970.

Selliah, S.: *The Self-Employed Women's Association, Ahmedabad*, Geneva, ILO, 1989.

Shanti, S.: *Varna, Castes and Scheduled Castes: A Documentation in Historical Perspective With a Classified Index to Scholarly Writings in Indian Journals (1890-1990)*, New Delhi, Concept Pub Co., 1991.

Singh, Kirpal: *Select Documents on Partition of Punjab — 1947, India and Pakistan*, Delhi, National Bookshop, 1991.

Singh, S.: *Women's Studies in India. Information Sources, Services and Programmes*, New Delhi, Sage, 1993.

Talib, G. S.: *Muslim League Attack on Sikhs and Hindus in the Punjab 1947*, New Delhi, SGPC, 1991.

Tinker, I.: *Persistent Inequalities: Women and World Development*, New York, OUP, 1990.

Viitanen, A.: *Invisible Hands. Women in Home-based Production*, New Delhi, Sage, 1987.

Vyas, A. & Singh, S.: *Women's Studies in India. Information Sources, Services and Programmes*, New Delhi, Sage, 1993.

INDEX

R

S

T

V

W

□□□